THE
SPIRITUAL
FOREST

THE
SPIRITUAL
FOREST

Timeless Jewish Wisdom for a Healthier Planet
and a Richer Spiritual Life

ANDY BECKER

PRAISE FOR THE SPIRITUAL FOREST

"Andy Becker has created another inspiring book that brings us closer to nature and to the spiritual side of life. Trees are the source of our physical sustenance but also serve as the quintessential Jewish metaphor for Torah in all its aspects. Read this book a bit at a time and you will be elevated to new levels of holiness."

Rabbi J.L. Mirel
Author of *Stepping Stones to Jewish Spiritual Living*

"This compact and wonderfully illustrated book brings readers a fresh perspective on why humans value and protect the arboreal world through the lens of rigorous religious scholarship and references, but with a light touch, evoking a nod of familiarity and conviction on every page. As a forest scientist who seeks ways to heighten the appreciation and conservation of trees, I will share this book near and far—to people of all experiences and faiths."

Nalini M. Nadkarni
Professor, School of Biological Sciences, University of Utah

"Andy Becker has done it again! This author has a habit of writing books that are spiritual, informative, and absolutely amazing. This time, it's *The Spiritual Forest*, and just as I was thinking, 'That's enough spiritual reading for the day,' Becker comes out with the astonishing idea that Adam may have been the first forest ranger. That's what he says!! This slender volume is not just a joyous hymn to the precious gift that trees are to the planet, but to myself—I have a picture in my mind of Adam in the Garden of Eden wearing his Smoky Bear hat and nothing else. You've got to read this book!"

Dorothy Wilhelm
Columnist, Broadcaster, Bestselling Author

"Andy Becker and I were high school friends and celebrated the first ever Earth Day together! He clearly still loves the earth and captures writing about why we need to take care of the earth from his Jewish tradition. Andy says, 'The actions we take to cultivate and guard trees are a service, not just to nature, but to humanity and creation.' I love how he writes from that remarkable notion and loved reading this book. Really nicely done and fun to read!"

Geoffrey L. Haskett
President, National Wildlife Refuge Association
Former US Fish and Wildlife Service Alaska Regional Director
Former US Polar Bear Commissioner
Former US Chief of the National Wildlife Refuge System

"*The Spiritual Forest* is many things: a spiritual guide, thoughtful prose, enlightening, encouragement, a call to arms (or shovels), but one thing it should never be is read quickly. This journey of reflection should be savored, like a feast that has been grown in one's private garden, harvested by hand, and prepared for friends. Throughout the well-crafted pages, it offers the reader an opportunity to ponder, provides resources for action, and most importantly, presents the need to look at our involvement and relationship with mother earth, the tree of life, from a different vantage point. Beautiful in its simplicity, each chapter melds the wisdom of the sages throughout time to one sole purpose, man's responsibility to protect nature and to teach the next generations to do the same. Exceptional and inspiring!"

"Just as others planted for me, I plant for future generations." – Talmud

Denise Frisino
Author/Speaker

"*The Spiritual Forest* is an inspiring and beautifully written work celebrating the preciousness of the earth and its glories. The vision is supported by a wide array of deep sources, drawn from both Jewish and non-Jewish traditions, along with practical suggestions for how to meaningfully contribute to the wellness and sustainability of our sacred home."

Rabbi Miles Krassen
PlanetaryJudaism.org

"Andy Becker makes a compelling spiritual case for environmentalism, without being preachy. Drawing from biblical passages, prophets, and sages, he shows rather than tells how the fate of our natural resources depends as much on our morality as our ingenuity. *The Spiritual Forest* inspires us to become long-term partners with nature."

Chris Bowman
Environmental Journalist

"It is a truly enriching experience to read Andy Becker's recent book, *The Spiritual Forest*. It provides a biblical basis for our responsibility to care for, nurture, and sustain our beautiful planet."

Graeme P. Berlyn, Ph.D.
E. H. Harriman Professor of Anatomy & Ecophysiology of Trees,
Yale School of the Environment

"As a man who has covered eight bare acres with a wide variety of trees over fifty years, and prefers to spend his Sunday mornings walking among them in my home-grown church, Andy Becker's *The Spiritual Forest* is the perfect biblical companion.

"It is a book to be read and absorbed slowly, perhaps sitting under a different leafy tree with each visit, contemplating the thoughts of Adam, the original park ranger, or Abraham, optimistically planting a tree in the desert.

"Each chapter brings more insight; personal change starts from within; our needed sustainability in a polluted world; the many blessings of fruit trees; the need to hold ourselves accountable in all situations; the utter joy in planting a tree and being able to sit quietly in its shadow in peace and happiness."

Bob Hill

Retired Book Author, Columnist, and Feature Writer with the *Louisville Courier-Journal*

"Few authors can weave spirituality, conservationism, and principled, value-based living together as masterfully as Andrew Becker in *The Spiritual Forest*. Becker writes in clear and colloquial language that allows his philosophies, which are primarily based on Judaism, to permeate the hearts and minds of the staunchest pragmatists and devoted congregations at the same time. *The Spiritual Forest* is yet another book in the *Spiritual Gardener* series that resonates with a wide breadth of audiences and begs readers to slow down, notice the physical world around them, and consider deepening their relationship to the earth."

Christina Vega

Author of *Still Clutching Maps* and Publisher at Blue Cactus Press

"If you have ever wondered why God would create millions of unique and wondrous species—and then encourage us to wipe them out—Andrew Becker's *The Spiritual Forest* may enlighten you. According to Andrew, that was never God's plan at all, just our misguided interpretation of the commandment, 'Go forth and conquer the world!' Using our relationship with trees as a metaphor for how we interact with all of nature, Andrew Becker suggests that we *can* achieve a sustainable relationship with Mother Nature if we only extend the same reverence we reserve for spirituality to the natural world that supports us. Good advice indeed!"

Douglas Tallamy, Ph.D.

TA Baker Professor of Agriculture & Natural Resources
Department of Entomology and Wildlife Ecology
University of Delaware

The Spiritual Forest

Timeless Jewish Wisdom for a Healthier Planet and a Richer Spiritual Life
The Spirtual Garden Series

Andy Becker

Published by Tree of the Field Publishing
www.AndyBecker.Life

TREE OF THE FIELD
—— PUBLISHING ——

ISBN: 978-1-7336698-7-0

OTHER BOOKS BY ANDY BECKER

The Spiritual Gardener

Insights from the Jewish Tradition to Help Your Garden Grow

The Kissing Rabbi

Lust, Betrayal, and a Community Turned Inside Out

Cracking An Egg

Childhood Stories

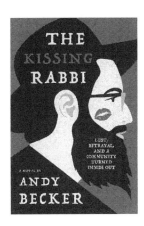

See Andy Becker's website and sign up for his newsletter at: andybecker.life

In memory of my parents, who introduced me to camping in the forests of the Pacific Northwest, and to my wife and children, with whom I have shared similar experiences. I can't wait to go camping with my grandchildren!

CONTENTS

INTRODUCTION

Even if I knew that I would die tomorrow, I would still plant an apple tree today.

– HILLEL THE ELDER

Did you ever think that Adam, Judaism's description of the first human being, might be called the world's first forest ranger? *The Spiritual Forest* proposes that fundamental spiritual values harmonize with modern concepts of environmentalism. While many traditions around the world embrace the natural world within their spiritual philosophies, this book draws on one religious tradition, Judaism, with quotations from the Torah,[1] Talmud,[2]

---

1   In Judaism, the Torah is the Holy Scriptures, the first five books of Moses.
2   The Talmud is the collection of Jewish law and tradition consisting of the Mishnah and the Gemara. The Mishnah is also known as the oral Torah, a major work of rabbinic literature. The Gemara consists of rabbinic commentary on the Mishnah, forming the second part of the Talmud.

Midrash,[3] Ethics of the Fathers,[4] and Chassidic Masters[5] to explore this universal relationship.

Have you ever considered a biblical basis, a fundamental underpinning, or a spiritual source for a love of trees, the forests, and the environment? Is there a spirituality within you that connects to nature, whether religious or not? How do you connect to the earth's trees and forests?

The great Chassidic masters often wrote of their spiritual connections to the forest and their love of trees. Their writings underscore the important biblical sources for an environmental ethic. Members of today's Jewish environmental movement, often called Jewcologists, have drawn from these sources to emphasize the importance of trees, forests, and the environment. The Baal Shem Tov, the great founder of the Chassidic movement, frolicked in the forests of Eastern Europe as a child. There, he connected to a level of holiness and spirituality that went unsurpassed. As an adult, he traveled from town to town to seed a forest of wisdom that we may now access by reading sacred texts and commentaries.

This attainable spirituality is also a call to action. Now, more than ever, what is left of our trees and forests remains under assault from fires, agricultural practices, urban expansion, and excessive logging. The earth's scientists keep sounding an ever-louder

3   A Midrash is a commentary on scriptures.
4   Ethics of the Fathers is a compilation of ethical teachings and maxims from rabbinic Jewish tradition.
5   A Chassid is a pious person who fulfills his or her duties towards God beyond what is commanded and obligatory.

alarm. Our forests are shrunk, burnt, and disappearing. The planet is on fire. The air we breathe is polluted.

Our problems with the environment are self-inflicted. We can reverse this disastrous trend. We must all pound the drum of environmentalism and encourage everyone—individuals, organizations, businesses, and governments—to plant and protect trees in line with proven environmental and traditional Native practices that will keep our forests and the earth healthy.

One important step to cultivate and guard our trees and forests is to recognize that they form part of our source for life itself. Here, we explore why the Torah and its most observant adherents through the ages so frequently discussed and honored trees.

So, how *do* we connect to the earth's trees and forests? Let's start by exploring our spiritual interconnectedness to nature; specifically what Jewish tradition teaches about trees and what we care about most—our health and well-being. Then we can consider what to do individually and collectively to turn our thoughts into actions. Shouldn't we all be environmentalists and Jewcologists, regardless of politics, religious affiliation, or background? I hope that this meditative read will help you answer that question with an enthusiastic, resounding, and unequivocal, "Yes!"

ADAM'S MISSION, OUR MISSION

(Cultivate and Guard)

See to it that you do not spoil and destroy My world, for if you do,

there will be no one else to repair it.

– MIDRASH KOHELET RABBAH 7:13

Did God ask Adam to serve as the first park ranger for *Gan Eden*, the Garden of Eden? Was Adam our first environmentalist and nature lover?

The Old Testament first describes God's creation with the highest of fanfare, to include vegetation, seeds, trees, and fruit. The text reads, "God said, 'Let the earth be covered by vegetation, plants that reproduce by seeds and trees (with edible bark that tastes like) fruit of their own species containing their own seed, over the earth!'—and that is what happened."

Of note, the vegetation, seeds, trees, and fruit precede human beings in the order of creation. The purpose of vegetation and trees, to support each other, to grow and to propagate, to fulfill their natural cycles, is unspoken. A plant or a tree's natural cycle is baked into its DNA. A plant or tree only needs favorable natural conditions to fulfill its best destiny. No further explanation is required.

However, in the story of creation, the mission of humanity is explicitly spelled out: "God, Almighty God, (persuaded) the man (to enter the Garden), and settled him in the Garden of Eden *to cultivate it and to guard it*." [Italics added.] Thus, Adam's mission, to take care of the Garden, to protect it against damage or harm, to help it flourish, and to keep it safe, is not unspoken, but fully and clearly declared.

God also underscored the importance of Adam's mission and issued a warning in this famous Midrash: "See My Works, how beautiful and praiseworthy they are. And everything that I created, I created it for you. Be careful not to spoil or destroy My World—for if you do, there will be nobody to repair it" (Midrash Kohelet Rabbah 7:13).

God did not tell Adam to chop down trees with abandon, to spray pesticides, and to compact, degrade, and erode the soil. God did not tell Adam to slash and burn, pollute the air, and float garbage patches of plastic, debris, and chemicals in the ocean. God tells Adam just the opposite. God, emphasizing the resplendence of the natural world, warns

Adam to be careful, and not to spoil God's creation, because once destroyed it cannot be fixed. Thus, God commands in both the positive, "to cultivate and to guard" and in the negative, "do not spoil or destroy."

The trees that covered the earth when God creates humanity were undoubtedly the greatest tapestry of natural art imaginable. The words of Genesis underscore the importance of the natural world and the imperative to care for vegetation and trees with God's mandate to Adam. The consequence of doing otherwise, of spoiling God's creation, is also made plain. If nature is despoiled and destroyed, nature cannot be repaired.

Why would Adam need to be persuaded to enter the Garden of Eden, the most desirable and miraculous place imaginable, a garden of wonder and delight, created specifically for human beings?

According to Rashi, one of the most revered rabbinical sages of yesteryear, God enticed Adam to enter the Garden with "pleasant words." Why would Adam need to be persuaded to enter the Garden of Eden, the most desirable and miraculous place imaginable, a garden of wonder and delight, created specifically for human beings? God even tells Adam the Garden is beautiful and praiseworthy. Isn't that readily apparent? Wouldn't the Garden's natural beauty attract Adam without any encouragement?

Perhaps the Garden's beauty was so breathtaking that it also instilled fear and awe. What was the nature of that fear? Adam's reluctance to enter the Garden meant he intuited the sanctity of the divine mission that God commanded him to undertake. The responsibility was so heavy, it created a hesitation, a feeling of timidity. It created self-doubt. Adam worried whether he was up to the task. Adam must have asked himself, "How can I, one mere human, care for something so beautiful, so natural, and so overwhelmingly glorious?" Adam did not yet understand the pleasure of divine service. God's pleasant words were necessary to explain that there was no greater way to experience joy and completeness in relation to God than to cultivate and guard the natural world that God created.

The aesthetics of vegetation and trees are undeniable. The many colors of the vegetation soften the majesty of the trees. We marvel at the irregularity of a single tree or their grouping together as a cluster, orchard, or forest. We are in awe of the tree's longevity. When we walk in the shadows of trees, we feel the peace of our surroundings and the majesty of creation ongoing all around us. A forest's soft trail leads us through holy ground, the greatest synagogue God ever created.

Trees store carbon dioxide, produce oxygen, absorb, purify, store water and minerals, prevent erosion, curb flooding, and reduce global warming. Trees are immensely important habitats for insects, birds, lichens, mammals, support a rich biodiversity of wild plants, and an astounding array of flora and fungi.

The botanists who specialize in plant anatomy study the intricacies of a tree's organizational hierarchy—the roots that anchor and absorb nutrients, leaves lifted into the light by supportive stems to allow for photosynthesis, and the microscopic structures within that organization. Water seeks its own level in nature, always running downhill, but in trees water conduction occurs in an upward direction. While wood is opaque and heavy, standing barren during a winter's sleep, leaves are thin and translucent, awakening and regenerating each spring.

Trees are the foremost representative of the natural world, and, in many regions, are absolutely necessary for a healthy and sustainable environment.

How do we cultivate and guard trees? Sometimes, we feel like we don't know what to do. The readily observable environmental devastation that we see in today's world is depressing and deflating. We feel overwhelmed. I'm just one person, we tell ourselves. What can one person do, we ask? Just like Adam, perhaps we are filled with self-doubt that we aren't up to the task.

First, we embrace the mission. We hug trees. We care about trees. We talk about trees. We feel reverence for trees. We raise consciousness about trees. We join organizations that push for reforestation. We plant trees.

If so inclined, we can seek a relationship with the divine in nature. We can connect to nature and feel closer to our own spirituality. When we plant trees, we feel the pleasure of contributing to the same mission divinely afforded to Adam in the bible.

Also, we understand that the actions we take to cultivate and guard trees are a service, not just to nature, but to humanity and creation. We understand that caring for and cultivating trees is a pleasant service, just like Adam's task. No matter where we find ourselves in our own spiritual forest, we find joy and satisfaction when we perform a generous task that benefits and sustains humanity by helping the environment. To support a healthy environment for human life, we recognize that trees play a central role.

The mission to cultivate and guard the Garden is oft-ignored. What would our earth look like if we restored our home, planet earth, into a beautiful garden? This societal and individual mission could be accepted pleasurably, not as a burden. What pleasant words can I offer myself and others to plant a tree? To lessen my own ecological footprint? To grow and care for our garden?

Humanity, guided by spirituality and science, can unite in this mission. We have the freedom to choose health over disease, clear waters over a cesspool, what's verdant over the barren, and redemption over destruction. If you are looking for biblical support for what needs to be done, it is there, front and center, unambiguous, with pleasant words.

- Do I care about the environment? Do I care about trees?
- What can I do on a daily level to become more environmentally aware?
- If I belong to a church, temple, synagogue, or mosque, is there an opportunity to reduce my organization's carbon footprint?

- If I belong to a group, is there an opportunity to improve our environmental awareness and sustainability?
- Should I start a garden?
- Should I plant a tree?

THE TAMARISK OF BE'ER SHEVA

(Hospitality and Persuasion)

All beginnings are difficult.

– RABBI ISHMAEL, TALMUD

How do we convince anyone of anything these days, let alone an increased focus on environmentalism? The blare of discourse seems to numb our senses and overwhelm us. Opinions are sliced, diced, and polarized into this side or that.

In Judaism, we are told to look to our patriarchs for guidance. The great Jewish sages tell us that each of the Jewish patriarchs exemplified important qualities that every human being should pattern him or herself after. Abraham epitomized outreach. How did he fulfill his mission? Through hospitality, charity, and kindness, actions we should challenge ourselves to emulate.

In the Sidra of Vayeira,[6] Genesis 21:33, Abraham's wanderings and sojourns end in Canaan, the promised land. His mission was to spread monotheism in a world full of idolatry. Can you imagine a more difficult task in a world of long-standing, passionate, and zealous idol worship? Avimelech, the King of the Philistines, recognized Abraham's miraculous salvation from Sodom, victory in war, and fatherhood in old age, and thus offered Abraham land where he could live in peace in the land of the Philistines. The peace covenant between the two leaders took place where Abraham dug a well; thus, the place was named Be'er Sheva, "well of the oath," after the peace pact. Abraham lived there in peace and security for many years.

Abraham's first act in Be'er Sheva, an area of desert, was to plant an *eschel*, a tamarisk tree. He planted the tree to provide shade from the brutal sun for strangers. What better way to spread and communicate his belief in monotheism than to do so while he provided hospitality and kindness, shade and shelter, to hot and tired travelers of the desert? Abraham invited strangers to rest, cool off, drink, and eat, only asking in return that they join him in learning to recognize the one source of their blessings.

Inherent in all of us is the natural and selfish desire to provide for ourselves and our

6   A Sidra is the weekly portion of the Torah read in the synagogue on the holy Sabbath.

children. However, when we plant a tree, we also provide all the benefits of that tree to everyone, including absolute strangers. In our heart of hearts, every human being would like to show generosity not just to himself or herself or his or her own family and circle of friends and relatives, but to everyone. Planting a tree is an act of kindness and a benefit to everyone.

The act of planting a tree may not feel necessary or logical. The act may surpass reason and intellect because it does not involve an immediate material payoff. Yet, the act of planting a tree, which may give an unknown person pleasure or improve another person's welfare, is a spiritual bonanza. The tree, like a tamarisk, may grow deep roots and also spread long lateral roots, even in a desert. The tree's aesthetic qualities may be enjoyed by any passerby. Like the tamarisk, it may store water, lessen soil erosion, and cycle minerals out of the ground through its beautiful leaves. The tree's benefits to all may last for many, many years and often outlive the planter.

Planting a tree symbolizes putting down roots, connecting to the earth, and caring about the present and the future. It is a direct commitment to the environment and helps to cool the earth.[7]

> *Planting a tree symbolizes putting down roots, connecting to the earth, and caring about the present and the future.*

7   See, www.epa.gov heatislands: trees and vegetation lower surface and air temperatures by providing shade and through evapotranspiration; trees are a proven way to reduce urban heat islands.

Abraham's methods of persuasion provide lessons to us all. We wish to save our planet from spiraling into destruction, but we may want more than that. We may wish to transform our planet into a garden. We can reach out to others with hospitality, kindness, and generosity. We can provide an example to ourselves, our families, and strangers. We can start with introspection, refining our own actions, educating ourselves, and we can start with the simple act of planting a tree.

Of course, emulating Abraham's many acts of hospitality to fulfill our own purpose in life does not mean mechanically trying to copy what worked for Abraham thousands of years ago. As stated in *Pirkei Avot*, Ethics of the Fathers, "You are not obligated to complete the work, but neither are you free to desist from it" (2:21). The sages also tell the story of Reb Zusha of Anapoli, whose students found him crying when he was close to death. They tried to comfort him, telling him that he was wise like Moses and kind like Abraham, so he was certain to be judged well in the heavenly court. Reb Zusha told his disciples, "When I appear before the heavenly court in judgment, they're not going to ask me, 'Zusha, why weren't you as great as Abraham, Isaac, or Jacob?' They're going to ask me, 'Zusha, why weren't you like Zusha? Why weren't you the best Zusha you could possibly be?'"

It's often not easy behaving differently, especially if it's something we've never done before. How do we break down a barrier within ourselves? Improving ourselves is often a big challenge. Simply put, sometimes just a tiny step in the right direction gets us going.

Like Zusha, we should try to be our best selves. Our capacity to be kind might start with our relationship with nature. To invite the garden into our lives, we might start by the simple kindness of planting a tree, then another, and another. Our own attempts at generosity will lead to the generosity of others. Our hospitality towards others will attract interest and will be welcomed by friends and strangers alike. Our powers of persuasion are best accomplished with very kind actions—like planting trees.

- What are the most common native trees where I live?
- Where can I plant a tree?
- Does my community have any tree planting programs or events?
- When is the best time to plant a tree in my area?

ROOTS

(Knowing from Whence We Came)

When the root is deep, there is no
reason to fear the wind.

– AFRICAN PROVERB

Much of the dispiritedness, stress, and confusion that we feel in this day and age is accentuated when we lose our connection to the natural world. The sages explain that the wicked person is cursed—that he will be, as stated in Psalms, "like tumbleweed, like straw before the wind." Does wickedness invade our psyches simply because we are dispirited, stressed, and confused? Who can concentrate when we are blown this way and that by the latest fashion or selfish impulse? Often, we don't have a mission, and often, we are not contributing to the health of the flora and fauna that surrounds us. We don't feel healthy, wealthy, or wise. Regardless of our age, we are dried out, cut off from the nourishment that we seek, rotting.

In contrast, trees are rooted to their spot, and even though they continue to grow every year, they preserve their past, and their past remains part of them. When we look at the rings within the trunk of a tree, we see that the tree has not transformed itself into something new and different each year, but that its history is recorded in its layers, while new layers are added. The past is gone, but the tree is still the tree, growing new branches and reaching new heights, with its past physically internalized within it.

Like trees, human beings, are from the earth and dependent upon it; however, if we negligently cut ourselves off from our past, from our connection to nature, we suffer a severe disconnect; we lose our identities. Our roots are in nature. The best way to grow might include a connection to our roots.

When our physical growth ends, we need not decline as a person. Just as the fruit of an old tree is as plentiful and as tasty as its younger cousin, human beings who are connected to their roots, and who realize who they are, can continue to be fruitful for a very long time. Perhaps, even long enough until the time comes to fall over, decay, and go back to the earth, to fertilize the next cycle of greenery.

The most obvious difference between a rock and all animals and plants, including human beings and trees, is that the rock will shrink in size over time due to erosion.

A rock, unlike living things, does not grow. Human beings and trees begin life as a single fertilized egg. Human beings reach a predetermined physical size, inherited in large part from parents. Trees, on the other hand, only constrained by their genetic make-up, grow to an indeterminate size proportional to the light, minerals, water, and oxygen in the specific environment. When left untouched and given the opportunity, the tree, due to the tree's roots, will not reach a predetermined size.

In fact, the root system of a tree, despite being tethered to one spot and being buried in the dark, moist earth, harmonizes with its branches and leaves. The roots of the tree create this harmony notwithstanding many potential challenges to its system, including grubs, microorganisms, including some fungi and bacteria, and rocks that block its movement. Our spiritual growth and refinement as human beings and as a human race is similarly not predetermined. Our potential for growth is unchartered, but only if we can live in harmony with nature, and understand the implications of our connection to our own roots. We can learn from tree roots what that means.

Tree roots do three things: (1) anchor the tree in the earth, (2) absorb what the tree needs to live—water and minerals, and (3) store excess food for future needs. Some large trees, like ones in a tropical rain forest, have roots near the surface that spread and create a broad base to support the trunk. The roots of these trees collect minerals and ions from the decomposing forest floor before torrential rains wash away nutrients. Forest trees in temperate zones are usually anchored by taproots that grow large horizontal branches in a wide circle, beyond the canopy of the branches and leaves. There, the root tips reach a drip zone, where the water is channeled by the tree.

The strength of tree roots is amazing and commonly evidenced when we see concrete sidewalks lifted and cracked or buried pipes crushed. Root systems and the architecture of trees below the surface can be extremely complex. Likewise, the anatomy of the roots, starting with root hairs that absorb water, and continuing with the components of root systems that transport water and nutrients upwards to other parts of the tree, is extraordinary.

What is buried and invisible in the human being are layers of the human psyche where subconscious feelings and urges, synapses triggering our intellect, and a spiritual soul coalesce to impact how we grow as people. Our roots, if undamaged and allowed to spread, permit us to blossom with a healthy identity and a sustainable, productive mission. Our roots are in nature herself, and our dependence on water, minerals, and air should compel us to seek harmony with the natural world.

Our roots are in nature herself, and our dependence on water, minerals, and air should compel us to seek harmony with the natural world.

Just like a tree, our roots are also dependent upon and derived from our connection to our Creator and the earth. Our roots feed the sustenance and the wellsprings of our very lives. The consequence of a good root system is a well-developed trunk, branches, and leaves—resulting in healthy growth and long life. We are healthiest and spiritually wealthiest when we are connected to the earth and continue to develop and grow, never resting on our laurels. Just as the sap of the tree continues to provide its nutrition as the tree matures, the blood coursing through our veins flows continuously throughout our lifetimes. A mature fruit tree continues to accomplish its purpose and bear fruit year after year. We can do the same.

- Did you know that tree roots can keep growing for years after a tree has been cut down?
- To what places or people in your past do you feel most rooted?
- What is it like when you feel disconnected from nature?
- Have you read about the natural history of the area where you live?

RABBI NACHMAN'S FOREST

(Solitude and Oneness)

Grant me the ability to be alone. May it be my custom to go outdoors each day among the trees and grasses among all growing things and there may I be alone, and enter into prayer to talk with the One to whom I belong.

– RABBI NACHMAN OF BRESLOV

Do we tend to overindulge in our self-interests, leading to a sense of separateness? Absorbed in our sense of self, do we lack concern for the interconnectedness of life and the ongoing creation that surrounds us? It seems our self-centeredness allows us to ignore our collective destiny with all living things. Sometimes, we fail to think about what is important. If we focus with such enormous concentration on narratives about ourselves, do we close our eyes to the light that illuminates what's positive in our world?

In this state of disconnectedness, we participate in a market, often by rote, which depletes natural resources and pollutes our earth, water, and air. We line our pockets with money at the expense of the environment. We suffer a passive dispiritedness, a collective malaise and hopelessness. Meanwhile, our nationalistic fears fuel our stockpiling of nuclear weapons. As we threaten each other with nuclear war, we fund proxy wars, one genocidal tragedy after another. Violence, egotism, and greed rule the day. Without much concern for the living things that co-inhabit the planet, we continuously exploit what we find in nature, like locusts devouring everything in their path.

Rabbi Nachman of Breslov, a *tzaddik gadol*, a righteous man of his generation (and the great-grandson of the founder of the Chassidic Movement, the Baal Shem Tov), famously said, "If you believe breaking is possible, believe fixing is possible." In other words, we are not condemned to self-centeredness, fear, neurosis, and malaise. He believed that changing a person's perception is achievable in the intuition available to every human being. It is beyond argument that change starts from within and everyone benefits from self-examination, but the question is how to make that happen. Perhaps, just taking a single step in a new and right direction may serve as a breakthrough. How do we do that?

Rabbi Nachman recommended getting off the beaten path, far away from the hustle and bustle of people, and as close as possible to nature. He famously prayed, "Grant me the ability to be alone. May it be my custom to go outdoors each day among the trees and grasses, among all growing things and there may I be alone, and enter into prayer to talk with the One to whom I belong." He said, "Find a day for yourself—better yet, late at night. Go to the forest or the field . . . You will meet solitude there. There you will be able to listen attentively to the noise of the wind first, to birds singing, to see wonderful nature and to notice yourself in it . . . and to come back to harmonic connection with the world and its Creator."

The idea of unity with the universe is essential if the human being is to cease and desist damaging the environment, and for realizing that each human being, and every non-human living animal and plant, are part of the natural world. Isn't this a consciousness attainable by everyone? A person needs solitude to experience nature and to optimize this realization. A simple hour of solitude in the forest imbues a sense of oneness with creation.

In many settings, we can practice meditation, biofeedback, breathing, visualization, positive speech, exercise, and relaxation, all means to somewhat the same ends. The

Rabbi Nachman recommended getting off the beaten path, far away from the hustle and bustle of people, and as close as possible to nature.

psychological, physical, and spiritual benefits of these practices are beyond argument. These techniques lend themselves to a meditation room, the gym, walking by the riverside with earbuds or without, or a psychologist's office. However, once one leaves the immediate influence of that space, the human condition allows the consciousness created there to dissipate quickly, like the air leaving a balloon.

Not so after an hour immersed in the forest. The solitude there, as Rabbi Nachman described, is like a glue adhering us to the natural world. There, we see and experience the preciousness of creation. Perhaps we cannot describe it, but we feel intuitively that we are standing in a vast space that puts our own importance and physicality into perspective. We recognize our responsibility to the majesty that surrounds us. We feel awe and reverence. This intuition of oneness is easiest to grasp surrounded by a forest, an eco-system older and more connected with the earth than humanity can understand in its towns and cities.

The Baal Shem Tov, the father of Chassidic Judaism, described the essential unity of life as a garment for Divine Oneness, years before a science of ecology was discovered. The Baal Shem Tov taught that a human being was not superior to other life in the universe. He put it to his disciples, "In what way is a human being superior to a worm? A worm serves the Creator with all of his intelligence and ability . . . In this sense, you are both equal in the eyes of Heaven. A person should consider himself, and the worm, and all creatures as comrades in the universe, for we are all created beings whose abilities are God-given." This comradeship, kinship, and interconnectedness with all of creation is a primary principle of ecology, the relationship of living things to their physical surroundings.

A towering disciple of the Baal Shem Tov, and the author of the *Tanya*,[8] Rabbi Shneur Zalman of Liadi, believed this perspective was essential to spiritual wellbeing. He wrote in the *Tanya*, "The essential thing . . . is to habituate your mind and thought constantly, so that it will be fixed in your mind and heart at all times, that everything your eyes see—heaven and earth and all they contain—all are 'outer garments' for the King, the Holy One, Blessed Be He. In this way you will constantly remember their inner dimension and their vitality."

If we follow Rabbi Nachman's recommendation to seek solitude and spirituality in the forest, we experience God's "outer garments" and our connectedness to the environment. Invariably, we also encounter two related qualities—humility and gratitude. Alone in the forest, we feel how small we are while developing a secure sense of self and an increased valuation of that which surrounds us. As we take in the forest, we unfailingly feel grateful for and appreciative of the gifts of nature.

To follow in the footsteps of Adam and his mission to guard the "outer garments," we must habituate our own inner dimensions with a determined focus to cultivate and guard

8   The Tanya is an early foundational work of Chassidic philosophy and mysticism authored by the founder of the Lubavitch movement, now known as Chabad.

nature and ongoing creation with thought, speech, and action. With our inner dimensions opened, activated, and vital, as full of sap as the inner parts of each tree of the forest, self-transformation is possible for everyone. As Rabbi Nachman of Breslov famously stated, "If you are not a better person tomorrow than you are today, what need have you for tomorrow?"

- Is there somewhere nearby where you can spend time in nature?
- When's the last time you visited a National Park or National Forest?
- How do you feel when you spend time in nature?
- How do you feel afterwards?
- How about joining a hiking or walking group?

SINGING TREES

(Elevating Our Use of Natural Resources)

For ye shall go out with joy, and be led forth with peace:
the mountains and the hills shall break forth before you into
singing, and all the trees of the field shall clap their hands.

– ISAIAH 55:12

A Midrash is a holy interpretation or commentary on a text in the Torah written long ago by learned sages. One important Midrash concerns a Psalm about when the trees of the forest sang with joy before God.

According to the Midrash, Jacob received a prophecy when he left Hebron in the land of Canaan and went to Egypt. He saw that his descendants would be commanded to build a *Mishkan*, a sanctuary or tabernacle, in the desert wilderness. For many years, as the Jews wandered in the desert and beyond, the *Mishkan*, built from acacia wood, served as the center of worship, lasting from the time of the Exodus through the rest of Moses's life, past the time the Jews crossed into the land of Israel, and up until King Solomon built the first Holy Temple in Jerusalem.

According to the Midrash, Jacob instructed his children to plant acacia trees in Egypt because of the prophecy. During the 400 years the Jews suffered slavery in Egypt, the saplings planted by Jacob's children grew into big trees. The Israelites cut down the trees at the time of the Exodus and carried them through the Sea of Reeds and into the wilderness for the purpose of building the *Mishkan*. When the Israelites cut down the acacia trees in Egypt in anticipation of building the *Mishkan*, the trees sang jubilantly before God. This Midrash derives from the Psalm that states, "Then all the trees of the forest will sing with joy before Hashem [God]."

The spiritual significance of the acacia trees relates both to their relationship with the Jewish people and their use. According to the last Lubavitcher Rebbe, Rabbi Menachem Mendel Schneerson, when the Jewish slaves in Egypt saw the acacia trees, it served as a link to Jacob's prophesy and their Jewish forefathers, the Patriarchs Abraham, Isaac, and Jacob. One medieval sage went so far as to posit that Adam took the trees from the Garden of Eden and gave them to Abraham who handed them down to his son Isaac, who then provided them to Jacob.

Jacob foresaw the enormous religious significance of planting the acacia trees. The transplanted trees from Jacob's native land paralleled the history of Jews going down into

Egypt. Thus, the connection of the acacia trees to the Patriarchs would be one cause for the trees to sing with joy as the Jews were finally freed from bondage to fulfill their destiny, becoming a monotheistic nation built on the laws and concepts of the Ten Commandments and the Torah. The acacia trees performed an integral role as a real-life manifestation of holiness during the restoration

Jacob foresaw the enormous religious significance of planting the acacia trees.

of the Jewish people. Although the wilderness that the Jews entered seemed inhospitable, the *Mishkan*, built from the trees that Jacob had the foresight to transplant was a tangible religious centerpiece for their journey to the land of Israel—on their road to redemption.

Further, the acacia wood used for the Tabernacle housed the holiest dwelling place for the Jews in the desert, facilitating their connection with the Divine. According to the Kabbalists, the vertical measurements of the pillars of the Tabernacle conformed to spiritual emanations. The acacia wood could not have been used for any holier purpose. The trees sang in jubilation when cut down as they were being used for the holiest of reasons.

Growing trees for a higher purpose, and then using the trees with respect and foresight, brings joy and jubilation to life. When we cut down trees, we need to do so to improve and elevate society, not to decimate nature. When we cut down trees, we are able to connect to our heritage and to our relationship with the trees and to nature. We can do so without acting blindly or without purpose or meaning.

The devil's advocate might argue that we are entitled to exploit natural resources as much as we like, for any reason, including selfish ones. After all, the argument goes, God instructed Adam and Eve to "fill the earth and subdue it, and rule over the fish of the sea, the birds of the sky, and every living thing that moves on earth." This argument is not only misguided, but spiritually bankrupt.

As stated sublimely by Rabbi Avraham Yitzchak Kook, "No intelligent thinking person could suppose that when Torah instructs humankind to dominate, it means the domination of a harsh ruler, who afflicts his people and servants merely to fulfill his personal whim and desire, according to the crookedness of his heart. It is unthinkable that the Torah would impose such a decree of servitude, sealed for all eternity, upon the world of God, Who is 'good to all, and His mercy is upon all His works' (Psalms 145:9), and Who declared, 'The world shall be built upon kindness' (Psalms 89:3)."

A Jewish ecologist, Ellen Bernstein, author of *The Splendor of Creation: A Biblical Ecology*, has examined in great detail the concept of the word "dominion" in the context of the word's derivation, meaning, neighboring words, and verses in the Bible, the historical context in which it was written, and interpretations over the course of the last 3,000 years. Her conclusion is that the concept of "dominion" is really a specific blessing or "bracha," "a divine act of love." Dominion, therefore, means that human beings are custodians of a gift, not owners of the land or nature, but its kindly and responsible preservationists. She aptly points out that we cannot own the land just as we cannot own the waters or the air, that the land belongs to everyone equally and in common. She wrote, "The blessing of mastery over the earth calls us to exercise compassion and wisdom in our relationship with nature so that the Creation will keep on creating for future generations."

If we employ this line of thinking, wasteful exploitation of our natural resources can be viewed as a blasphemous insult, an expression of ingratitude towards nature, creation, and God. Advocating for the ethical and purposeful use of our natural resources is not an anti-business attitude, but rather a spiritual and practical imperative. Human beings who decimate nature for invalid purposes engage in a form of gluttony that corrupts their souls. Self-interest, egotism, greed, and waste also exemplify a lack of humility. We need "to see the forest through the trees" with spirituality and greater awareness of the wonder and beauty of the earth's natural resources. When we cut down trees, we want the trees to sing with joy.

- Did you know that the Hawaiian Koa tree is an acacia that is prized for its wood and is used to make guitars and ukuleles? Koa was considered the wood of Hawaiian royalty and historically was used to build canoes, surfboards, and spear handles.
- Looking for songs that celebrate trees? Check out these links:

Lifegate.com

lyrics.com

rachelmcclary.com (preschool songs)

themusicalhype.com

maineaudubon.com

CEDAR TREE OH CEDAR TREE

(Sustainability)

*The wrongs done to trees, wrongs of every sort, are done in the
darkness of ignorance and unbelief, for when the light comes,
the heart of the people is always right.*

– **JOHN MUIR**, *JOHN OF THE MOUNTAINS:
THE UNPUBLISHED JOURNALS*

The Western Red Cedar of the Pacific Northwest, with its wonderful scent and dark evergreen splays of scale-like leaves, epitomizes the sacredness and beauty of the forest. The branches at the very top of the cedars look like drooping arms curving upward, like an orchestra conductor readying the rest of the forest to perform nature's symphony. Red cedars often reach ages of 800 to 1,000 years, and some in western Washington State are over 2,000 years old. The lower trunks flare out as the trees commonly grow up to 200 feet tall.

Native American tribes, including those of the Pacific Northwest, that practiced sustainable forestry, utilized cedar trees to make canoes and used their bark for clothing, ropes, blankets, mats, and baskets. The bark of the tree may be removed in long strips. Roots of the tree were even used for fishhooks. Majestic cedar totem poles depicting spiritual forces and important histories stand to this day. Red cedar wood has a wonderful long-lasting quality and is a natural insect repellent. No part of the tree was wasted by the indigenous people of the Pacific Northwest who fully knew its properties and qualities.

The Salish tribes, among others, used cedar leaves and bark medicinally, and associated the cedar tree with prayer, healing, dreams, and protection against disease. They believed that a weary traveler gained strength just by leaning against a cedar tree. The Salish were the first environmentalists of the Pacific Northwest. Their knowledge of natural resources let them use the cedar trees while not using them up.

This contrasts with the tremendous waste produced when Red Cedar was and continues to be clear cut for lumber, shake, and shingle sawmills. In the early 1890s, the cedar shingle industry grew as shingles were shipped overland by rail and by water on schooners. This resulted in over-logging. Old-growth Western Red Cedars were almost wiped out as companies like Macmillan-Bloedel made billions. Weyerhaeuser, which bought out Macmillan-Bloedel, now manufactures Western Red Cedar under the label *CedarOne* which they market as siding, decking, and outdoor furniture at big box stores like The Home Depot.

Red Cedar, when used as a building material, generates less water and air pollution than steel, plastic composites, and concrete. These other products require massive fossil fuel expenditures for production, releasing carbon dioxide into the atmosphere. Alternatively, Red Cedar can be grown with rain, soil, and sun, acting like a washing machine, using photosynthesis to suck toxins out of the air and provide atmospheric oxygen. Red Cedar is a renewable resource and can be grown in mixed stands with other trees, from sea level to high elevations, on mountain sides, and in forested swamps. The tree is shade tolerant and able to reproduce even under dense shade.

Further, if we are smart in our forestry practices with Red Cedar, we can prohibit the open burning of mill waste and instead produce inexpensive biofuel that can generate clean electricity. Weyerhaeuser has jumped on the biofuel bandwagon and claims that they use more than seventy percent of their energy from renewable biomass, thus reducing their air-polluting ways.

We have trouble imagining a world covered with forests when scientists agree that over 80 percent of these forests have either been destroyed or degraded in just the last

100 years. The Western Red Cedar is just one of many species of forest tree to suffer this catastrophe.

Sages and scholars remind us that the Bible mandated a green belt around every city, limiting urban sprawl, and allowing its inhabitants a constant vista of the natural world. The great rabbis of old also limited the grazing of livestock to avoid harm to the environment. Even King Solomon appointed a minister to limit the harvesting of wood in the forests.

Cedar trees worldwide also include the famous Cedars of Lebanon, which have also been significantly deforested. The Cedars of Lebanon should be an important example for us. As stated in the Psalms that the observant recite daily, "The righteous flourish like the palm tree, grow like the cedar in Lebanon . . . Even in old age they shall be full of sap and freshness." The righteous person is connected to his or her environment. That person will grow and has every opportunity to be productive as he or she matures.

So many people today experience a lack of connection between themselves and their surroundings. They don't feel rooted with any natural or spiritual relationship to their home. They are easily uprooted, which leads to feelings of alienation, detachment, and loneliness. Psalms underscores the point, stating that a rotten person is "like tumbleweed, like straw before the wind." The rotten person is, therefore, unable to put down roots, to commit to a mission or any kind of relevance. As such, that person feels directionless and undernourished, starved for meaning.

Worldwide deforestation continues at an alarming rate notwithstanding efforts at tree planting and reforestation in some areas. We can heal the loss of cedars in Lebanon, the loss of cedars in the Pacific Northwest, and the loss of cedars and every species of tree everywhere, through significantly increased efforts at sustainability. Sustainability means enlarging our existing forests. Sustainability means choosing and valuing our health and our lives. To maintain our ecological balance, to cool the planet, to protect and maintain our atmosphere, we need to stand up, stand tall, and stand strong, in favor of reforestation and advocating for trees everywhere. Let the cedar tree conduct its spiritual symphony in the coastal plain, shaded forest, swamp, or mountainside, and thus fulfill its purpose. Let us stand with our environment and flourish physically and spiritually. Let us grow individually and collectively like the Cedars of Lebanon, full of sap, full of energy, to cultivate and guard our precious world.

Let the cedar tree conduct its spiritual symphony in the coastal plain, shaded forest, swamp, or mountainside, and thus fulfill its purpose.

- Reduce, reuse, recycle
- Buy planet-friendly: for example, buy local and in season, buy used, use reusable shopping bags, use recycled packaging, and avoid pre-washed; See, greenerdeal. com or envivronment911.org

- #Plasticfree
- Check the label: look for Energy Star (for energy efficiency), USDA Organic Seal (for organic products), Forest Stewardship Council (for products made from trees in responsibly managed forests), and Green Seal (for general sustainability)
- Adopt a cedar tree: prune dead or damaged twigs and branches and remove the clippings, add 2-3 inches of mulch around the tree's base, water during dry periods if the tree appears to be browning

THE LORAXES

(The Importance of Education)

Education means teaching a child to be curious, to wonder, to reflect, to enquire. The child who asks becomes a partner in the learning process, an active recipient. To ask is to grow.

– RABBI LORD JONATHAN SACKS

Dr. Seuss wrote *The Lorax*, his personal favorite of all of his children's books, out of anger at corporate greed for destroying our old-growth forests. Recognized by the National Educational Association as one of the top 100 children's books for teachers, *The Lorax* tells the story of the "Once-ler's" need to keep "biggering" his business until his company chops down all the Truffula trees, despite the repeated warnings of the Lorax, who speaks for the trees.

As Seuss so creatively wrote and endearingly illustrated, the trees can't speak for themselves. Seuss taught a lesson that he wanted every child to understand: that unchecked greed will destroy our environment, turning what God created as *Gan Eden*, the Garden of Eden, into a wasteland. Prior to the arrival of the Europeans in the United States, half of the United States was forested. Our wilderness areas are now a fraction of what they once were. Even today, illegal logging, where companies regularly exceed the area granted by their permits, is an under-publicized national scandal. Illegal logging in many places in other parts of the world is even worse, a horribly critical disaster. Seuss' charming children's book taught that unchecked corporate greed will destroy our beautiful forests.

The spiritually observant knows who really owns the land. As stated in Psalms, "The earth is the Lord's and the fullness thereof." And as stated in Leviticus, "And the Land shall not be sold in perpetuity, for the land is Mine, for you are strangers and sojourners with Me." In other words, the land does not belong to us, but rather we belong to the land. Jewish tradition teaches that God's mandate to Adam "to cultivate and to guard" means that we must care for our precious earth to preserve what God created. Damaging the forests and our environment is an offense against what God created.

Every pre-school and elementary school might transform a sunny portion of its neglected landscaping

Every pre-school and elementary school might transform a sunny portion of its neglected landscaping into a working garden for the children.

into a working garden for the children. Children love to dig in the dirt. Children love nature and love being outside. Small, raised beds or even a few containers will suffice if there isn't much space. Planning the garden is a learning experience about the soil, the sun, and the seasons. When kids plant seeds, water the dirt, and see seedlings pop up and grow, it's exciting. They are relating to the soil and participating in the wonder of creation. Ultimately, they get to taste the bounty of their own labor. The cucumber that they grow will taste better than anything their family purchased from the store. Time in the garden lowers stress levels, promotes communication skills, and gives children a sense of respect and a love for the earth.

Likewise, many organizations, such as the Arbor Day Foundation, a non-profit dedicated to planting trees, will partner with schools and youth groups, religious and secular, to explore nature, learn about trees, and inspire kids and adults alike to plant, nurture, and celebrate trees. The Nature Conservancy acquires land and conservation easements worldwide, protecting and restoring forests. Their projects run the gamut, including volunteer activities for kids, and include their Plant a Billion Trees campaign, which they hope to complete by 2025. Nonprofit trails organizations in many states help volunteers build and maintain hiking trails, including taking high-schoolers on volunteer vacations to share nature and the outdoors. One of the most venerated environmental organizations, founded in 1892 by John Muir, is the Sierra Club, with a long history of fighting for preservation, parks, and wildlife. The Sierra Club's Student Coalition is a broad network of high school and college kids who work on campaigns to protect the environment.

Education is the key. Notwithstanding the many wonderful organizations and outstanding volunteers, all doing their best to be the Lorax and speak for the trees, our planet is in crisis. We need to expand the wonderful efforts of the nonprofits.

We can directly influence who we are and how we relate to our planet—how health and care for the environment are more important than greed—if we plant these seeds through the education of our children. Multiple opportunities abound to let young people learn actively rather than passively about nature and trees. We need to lessen the disconnect people feel to the earth and instill important values that will allow the next generation to choose life and ensure their own survival. We do not want to raise a generation of electronically addicted, neurotic, self-centered, stressed-out kids. If we expose children to nature in a caring and loving way, they can taste for themselves their connection to the land and attune to their higher purpose in life. As stated in Proverbs 22:6, "Educate the youngster according to his way, then, even when he grows old, he shall not depart from it." There is a Lorax in every one of us.

- Talk to the local elementary school principal about starting a garden on school grounds for the children. The garden might include tree seedlings native to the area that the children can take home and plant.

- Would the local high school biology teacher be willing to lead a field biology field trip?
- Interested in organizations that provide educational programs about trees? See the following links to get started:

    arborday.org

    preserve.nature.org

    act.sierraclub.org

THE GIANT SEQUOIA

(The Strength of Community)

*Never doubt that a small group of thoughtful, committed citizens can
change the world; indeed, it is the only thing that ever has.*
– MARGARET MEAD

*When we try to pick out anything by itself,
we find it hitched to everything else in the Universe.*
– JOHN MUIR, *MY FIRST SUMMER IN THE SIERRA*

Plants that are more primitive on the evolutionary scale than the ones that flower
are the gymnosperms (Greek: gymnos "naked"; sperma, "seed"). Unlike plants that have
a shell or outer covering around their seeds, these plants grow seeds in the open spaces

of cones and include all the conifers including cedar, redwood, juniper, cypress, fir, and pine. They do not bear fruit, and they propagate from spores that develop into pollen grains and ovules. The gymnosperms include the largest living plants on earth, the giant sequoias. A giant sequoia, *Sequoiadendron giganteum*, is a majestic tree that may live longer than many generations of human beings. A giant sequoia may live 2,000 to 3,000 years, continuing to grow throughout its life.

The giant sequoia was nicknamed the Big Tree by John Muir and is also known as the giant redwood and Sierra redwood.[9] These trees are native to the western slopes, riverbeds, and inland foothills of California's Sierra Nevada range. They are the world's largest trees and among the oldest living things on earth. Imagine an evergreen tree older than Abraham, Isaac, or Jacob—a tree that was already growing at the time of the giving of the Torah. You can visit such trees today in California.

The Big Trees stirred John Muir to famously write:

> *Do behold the King in his glory. King Sequoia! Behold! Behold! seems all I can say. Some time ago I left all for Sequoia and have been and am at his feet, fasting and praying for light, for is he not the greatest light in the woods, in the world? Where are such columns of sunshine, tangible, accessible, terrestrialized?*

9   The author fully endorses the Sierra Club's repudiation of John Muir's history of racism.

The giant sequoia is similar in many respects to California's coastal redwoods. Both have thick red bark that protects them from brush fires and insects. The coastal redwoods grow more slender than the sequoias and some grow taller. These redwoods grow along the coasts of California and Oregon where they luxuriate in morning fog and frequent winter rains.

In fact, as large and as tall as the sequoias and redwoods are, they grow close enough together that if you walk through a grove of these old giants, especially when cloaked in California or Oregon sunshine, the light diffuses so spectacularly that you will see that Muir was not unique in evoking the holiness of his experience. The same experience awaits anyone tiptoeing in awe among the giant sequoias and coastal redwoods, viscerally holier than entering any human constructs, including the oldest and greatest synagogues, cathedrals, or mosques presently standing or ever known to humankind. When you experience a grove of the mighty Big Trees, spirituality is not a concept to decipher from a prayer book or among old sacred papers. The beauty of the trees, their divinity, and their antiquity are palpable through the softness of the forest floor, the shafts of light, and the smell of the bark. The strength and height of these forest giants are all supernally internalized just by standing in their midst.

Interestingly, despite the enormous size of a giant sequoia, their seed cones are small, about an inch and a half to three inches long with seeds that grow on spiral scales, averaging 230 seeds per cone. A really big sequoia may have about 11,000 cones leading botanists to estimate that a mature giant sequoia may disperse 300,000 to 400,000 seeds per year. John Muir wrote, "Nature takes care, however, that not one seed in a million shall germinate at all, and of those that do perhaps not one in ten thousand is suffered to live through the many vicissitudes of storm, drought, fire, and snow-crushing that beset their youth."

Amazingly, the roots of the giant Sequoia and the California redwood are shallow, only going down about six to twelve feet at most for a mature tree; yet, these trees survive brutal winds, storms, fires, earthquakes, and flooding. The trees rarely topple over. Their roots, while shallow, spread wide, and are intertwined with those of their cluster, so the trees support each other.

A community can thrive, year after year, when its individual members hold each other up.

The giant sequoia and redwood represent the strength of community. The trees are connected by their roots. A community can thrive, year after year, when its individual members hold each other up. When we strengthen each other in our community, we can grow higher and higher, we can each reach towards the sun, and all benefit, spreading seeds each year, like hundreds of thousands of sparks of light.

The unity of the Jewish people—despite the destruction of the Holy Temple, the Diaspora, inquisitions, expulsions, pogroms, the holocaust, and constant attacks on the modern State of Israel—is based on the soul of every Jew being intertwined with that of every other Jew. While civilizations and great nations of the world have perished, one after another, century after century, the Jewish people have survived and thrived wherever and whenever allowed to live in peace, refining their spiritual growth throughout the generations to serve as a "light upon the nations." The strength of the Jewish people derives from their intertwined roots and their ability to hold each other up to fulfill their spiritual mission.

Another ironic parallel between the durability of the giant sequoia and the Jewish people concerns forest fires. When destructive forest fires sweep through a sequoia forest, the fire accelerates the release of seeds from the cones, recycles nutrients into the soil, and opens up holes in the forest canopy to allow sunlight to reach young sequoia seedlings. As Jews throughout history have faced violence and repression, Jews have perished or fled, often giving up everything, just to survive. What never perished were the souls of the Jewish people. Those Jewish souls, often spread far and wide, have "replanted" themselves over and over again with renewed dedication to their God and their community in all four corners of the world, repeatedly finding a minyan with which to pray,[10] and a steadfast dedication to the mission of healing humanity.[11]

10 A quorum of ten Jewish adults required for traditional worship in a synagogue.
11 The concept of Tikkun olam in Judaism is the idea that the individual is also responsible for repairing the world at large.

Like the giant sequoia, Jews, and all peoples for that matter, flourish more where they are allowed to grow together, even in exile. Material fortunes and bodily security may suffer awful risks, but the human soul is never exiled. It remains intact and intertwined as one with the soul of every other person, and the soul of humanity. The capacity of that intertwined soul is infinite, naturally seeks the light, and will never stop growing.

- When are you going to visit California's groves of giant sequoias?
- Plan your visit to Sequoia and Kings Canyon National Parks at nps.gov.
- Wish to donate to save these magnificent trees? Check out:

savetheredwoods.org

sequoiaparksconservancy.org

THOU SHALL NOT DESTROY THE TREES

(*Bal Tashchit* – Do Not Waste)

The concept known as bal tashchit – 'Do not destroy' – has a special significance in Jewish tradition . . . We are constantly being warned in our faith that the capricious, thoughtless, wasteful destruction of the elements and creatures of the earth is wrong . . . We should remind ourselves daily of our responsibility to all aspects of creation.

– DAVID GEFFEN

We universally possess a sense of right and wrong. Even as children, when we are too young to articulate an explanation, we already intuitively know right from wrong.

Our sense of right and wrong expands outward from our relationships in our nuclear family to relationships with others and becomes cemented as we enter a greater social contract with society. We learn from a young age and continue to learn into adulthood that we may not act solely absorbed in our self-interests, fueled by whim, anger, pride, or ego.

Included in our sense of right and wrong is our belief that wanton destruction and vandalism are sinful.

Included in our sense of right and wrong is our belief that wanton destruction and vandalism are sinful. On one end of the moral spectrum, vandalism and destruction are criminal. Examples include intentional, devilish acts that destroy or deface property, like "keying" a car or knocking over grave markers. Some intentional acts are extremely destructive and punished severely, like feloniously starting fires that burn down buildings.

On the other end of the same moral spectrum are wasteful acts, however small, that are also wrong. While these lesser acts may seem innocuous, like throwing away perfectly good food, littering, or failing to recycle, we know that these acts, even if only done carelessly, are also wrong.

In Deuteronomy, God provides the explicit commandment of *bal tashchit*—do not waste or destroy. The central focus of the commandment are fruit trees in times of war:

When you besiege a city for many days to wage war against it to capture it,
you shall not destroy its trees by wielding an ax against them, for you may
eat from them, but you shall not cut them down (Deuteronomy 20: 19-20).

Clearly, the commandment prohibits cutting down fruit trees during wartime. However, the Talmudic Rabbis and holy sages have consistently interpreted this verse much more broadly, deriving a general principle to extend far beyond the case of fruit trees during ancient wars. The Rabbinical logic was that a principle that applied during an extreme time, a time of war, should apply even more so during times of peace. This is a common form of Talmudic interpretation that draws down an idea, principal, or inference from a more severe case to a less severe case.

This begs the question, however, whether the prohibition against the destruction of fruit trees is based on commercial values, such as the scarcity of food in wartime, and is extended to property rights in peacetime, or is there a greater moral and spiritual underpinning consistent with the Torah's other lessons? Does *bal tashchit* provide us with an environmental mandate to apply in our daily lives?

The Talmudic and other Jewish sages interpreted the prohibition against waste and destruction to include wasting energy, water, and money; in short, against wasting *any* resources. The great Maimonides (1135-1204), a prolific and influential Torah scholar, astronomer, and physician, applied the prohibition to smashing household goods, tearing clothes, demolishing a building, stopping up a spring, or destroying food. Another sage criticized wasting water needed by others. Rabbi Joseph is quoted stating, "One should not spill water out of his pool at a time when others need it." Rabbi Moshe Aaron Poleyeff (1888-1967) wrote that overeating may be a double transgression of *bal tashchit* by wasting food and harming one's health, while a more modern Jewish scholar, Rabbi Shaya Karlinsky, posited that taking more food than one can eat at a buffet food line to also be *bal tashchit*. A thirteenth-century holy treatise, the *Sefer HaChinuch*, stated that the righteous, "do not allow the loss of even a grain of mustard, being distressed at the sight of any loss or destruction. If they can help it, they prevent any destruction with all the means at their disposal."

Thus, *bal tashchit* does not describe merely an economic principle, but a moral imperative. While the pious will not easily suffer the loss of a single seed "in the world," "the wicked rejoice at the destruction of the world." No lesser authority than Rebbe Shneur Zalman of Liadi (1745-1812) applied the law of *bal tashchit* to ownerless property. *Bal tashchit* is about morality and not limited to commercial values.

These many applications of *bal tashchit* emphasize that all resources are a creation of the Holy One. Thus, to use resources wastefully is an insult to God. We weren't created to destroy and waste, even though we habitually do so. We were created for a divine purpose which includes an environmental ethic. God gave us bountiful resources and beautiful fruit trees for a reason. Let us heed the commandment, "Thou shall not destroy the trees . . ."

and adopt conservation, environmentalism, and kindness toward our green, precious earth as a primary ethic in our everyday lives.

- Compost!
- Shop sustainably certified products.
- Avoid products containing palm oil.
- Support ecotourism: e.g., purchase local crafts, research your tour operator and accommodation, opt for public transportation, avoid plastic, respect wildlife.
- For more tips, see EPA.gov: Reducing Waste: What You Can Do.

BHUTAN AND ISRAEL

(Examples for Nations to Follow)

*During the twenty years since the first earth Day in 1970, the world
lost nearly 200 million hectares of tree cover, an area roughly the size
of the United States east of the Mississippi River.*

LESTER R. BROWN, PIONEER ENVIRONMENTALIST

*Between 15 million to 18 million hectares of forest, an area the
size of Bangladesh, are destroyed every year. On average 2,400
trees are cut down each minute.*

WIKIPEDIA.ORG, *DEFORESTATION*

Bhutan, a landlocked nation sandwiched between India and China in the eastern Himalayas, enshrined environmental conservation in its constitution. In Bhutan, 60 percent of the land is under forest cover, 40 percent of the land is comprised of protected areas, and 9 percent of the land provides for biodiversity corridors for phenomenally rich wildlife, including the golden langur, red panda, snow leopard, and barking deer. The country is fast achieving a farming industry that is 100 percent organic. When their king and queen gave birth to a baby prince, the people of Bhutan planted 108,000 trees as a birthday present. In 2015, 50,000 tree saplings were planted in Bhutan in just one hour, a world record. Bhutan is the only country on earth that is carbon negative, producing more oxygen than it consumes because of its thick blankets of green forests that wrap around its mountains, in contrast to so many countries that have denuded their hills.

The Buddhist reverence for trees may start with the Buddha's biography, as he was born under a sal tree, experienced intense spirituality for the first time under a rose-apple tree, and became enlightened under a *Ficus religiosa*, a sacred fig tree. Sacred trees may be found next to shrines and temples throughout Buddhist and Hindu countries. Worldwide, trees are symbols of long life, health, beauty, and compassion. The veneration of trees is not an invention of any one religion or culture. But perhaps Bhutan, with its rich Buddhist history, and because it was never colonized,

The veneration of trees is not an invention of any one religion or culture.

has succeeded in incorporating a pervasive and nationalistic love of trees in its vision for its future quicker and better than any other country.

Interestingly, Bhutan and Israel are very like-minded countries when it comes to planting trees. Jews in the diaspora and Jews in *Eretz Yisrael*, the land of Israel, have funded tree planting in Israel by putting money in a *pushke*, usually a little tin blue box kept in the kitchen, since the Jewish National Fund was founded with Theodore Herzl's support in 1901. By 2007, the JNF owned 13 percent of the total land in Israel and had planted over 240 million trees, built 180 dams and reservoirs, developed 250,000 acres of land, and established more than 1,000 parks.

The historic roots of charitable giving, which is called *tzedakah*, the Hebrew word for justice, derives from Leviticus and Deuteronomy, where passages command us to provide for others who are in need. Until Israel and every other nation of the world, other than Bhutan, become carbon neutral, all of us, members of every single country on the planet, need *tzedakah* to provide for reforestation, conservation, and land reclamation. Trees critically affect our climate, our air, and the cycle of all living things on earth, including human beings. Without trees, none of us would be here.

The Midrash teaches: "It is said, 'Follow the Lord, your God. This means follow His example. When He created the world, His first action was to plant trees, as it is written, 'And God planted a garden of trees in Eden.' So you, too, when you will enter the land of Israel, planting trees should be your first involvement." The sages who taught this

Midrash centuries ago would surely say an enthusiastic *"L'Chaim!"*[12] to the ongoing accomplishments of organizations like the JNF.

How hard is it to plant a tree where you live? If you live in the northern hemisphere, trees often respond well to plantings in their dormant season in the fall just after the leaves start to drop, or in early spring before the buds break out. It is easy to check to make sure that you are planting the right tree in the right place at the right time. In tropical climes, any time is often a good time to plant a tree. Like the royals of Bhutan, when a new member of your family is born, planting a tree to honor that child is a joyful experience. Any special occasion may merit putting another sapling in the ground such as a marriage, moving into a new house, a bar or bat mitzvah, or a college graduation. We can all feel like kings and queens when we plant a tree.

Rabbi Yochanan ben Zakkai used to say, "If you have a sapling in your hand and you are told that the Messiah has come,[13] first plant the sapling and then go and meet the Messiah." Rabbi Yochanan, who survived the destruction of the Second Temple in Jerusalem, understood the importance of planting each little tree. He understood that redemption required a patient, practical, laborious attention to detail and completion of the tasks at hand. As the sages tell us, the day is long and the tasks are many. Let's get to

---

12 *"L'Chaim!"* means "To Life!" A *"L'Chaim"* is usually a toast to a person's health and well-being.
13 The Messiah is the expected anointed king who would deliver the Jewish people from foreign bondage and restore the glories of its golden age.

work! If small countries like Bhutan and Israel can consistently dedicate themselves to planting trees, shouldn't all nations follow their example?

- Would you like to contribute to reforestation? Here are just a few links:

  onetreeplanted.org

  fs.usda.gov

  www.nature.org

  plantatreeproject.com

- Would you like to plant a memorial tree for a dearly departed loved one in Israel? See, shiva.com/trees-in-israel/jnf
- Want to join a tree planting party? There's probably one upcoming close to where you live. Just type "tree planting parties near me" in your browser.

KING APPLE

(Popularity)

Golden apples in silver dishes – such is a word in the right place.

– KING SOLOMON IN PROVERBS 25:11

Red Delicious, Cosmic Crisp, Gala, Fuji, Granny Smith, Honeycrisp, Golden Delicious, Cripps Pink, and Braeburn apples are grown in Washington State, all picked by hand, and shipped in one-hundred million boxes, each weighing around forty pounds, every year. How many apples is that? According to the Washington Apple Commission, that's upwards of *twelve billion* apples. The Commission says that if you put all of the apples picked in just one year in Washington State in a line, side by side, they would circle the earth twenty-nine times.

The apple's popularity derives from its virtues and the apple merits its nickname as the King of all fruits.[14] Apples grow all over the world, store and keep well, taste great, and smell wonderful. Apples come in many colors and shades of colors from red to green to gold. The apple's fruit is juicy enough to run down your chin and crunchy enough to clean your teeth. Flavors run the gamut from sweet to sour. Apples are kid-friendly, versatile, and healthy. Eaten raw or baked, they complement any meal from snacks to salads to desserts.

Apple growers in the United States are quick to trumpet that, "An apple a day keeps the doctor away," and the patriotic refrain, "As American as apple pie." Yet, apples are not native to North America. Botanists and genome scientists believe that apple trees (*Malus sieversii*) originated in Central Asia, specifically in Kazakhstan, Kyrgyzstan, Tajikistan, and Xinjiang, China, and were only brought to North America by colonists from Europe.[15] The apple tree is likely the first tree to be cultivated in Asia and Europe. Alexander the Great got the credit for "discovering" dwarf apples in Kazakhstan in 328 BCE. The British brought the apple to Boston, the Dutch to New York, and the French to Canada. Once in North America, apple seedlings were commonly advertised in nursery catalogs and spread quickly along trade routes and commonly planted on farms. The legend of Johnny Appleseed, a farm boy who wandered the Midwest with a bag filled with apple seeds, became part of the

14 A dear friend pointed out that the apple tree should be called Queen Apple as it develops from a ripened ovary and houses its seeds.
15 Wikipedia.org/Apple#History

country's lexicon. Eventually, rivers and dams allowed for extensive irrigation of farmlands, especially east of the Cascade Mountains, and King Apple became a multibillion-dollar industry in Washington State.

Jews dip slices of apples into honey on Rosh Hashanah as they wish each other a sweet New Year. King Solomon, referring to the love between the Jewish people and the Almighty, wrote in the Song of Songs, "Beneath the apple tree I aroused your love."

Other cultures and religions have also venerated the apple, including the Greeks and the Romans. Hercules, the greatest of the Greek heroes, was ordered to perform Ten Labors, which included picking golden apples off the Tree of Life to atone for slaying his wife and children. In other Greek mythology, Aphrodite used her beauty to claim a golden apple tossed into a wedding party, an act that contributed to the Trojan War.

> *Jews dip slices of apples into honey on Rosh Hashanah as they wish each other a sweet New Year.*

The apple is also commonly viewed as the forbidden fruit of the Tree of Knowledge of Good and Evil. This idea may originate because of a misunderstanding between the similarity in Latin of the words *malus* (evil) and *malum* (apple). Likewise, the part of our throat that sticks out is often called an Adam's apple from the misguided idea that the forbidden fruit got stuck in Adam's throat when he swallowed it. King Apple has been horribly defamed. The fact is that the Tree of Knowledge of Good and Evil is not named in Genesis. This is beyond argument. The only argument concerns the identity of the Tree.

The great Jewish sages of the Talmud offer varying opinions as to the identity of the Tree of Knowledge. None of the opinions include King Apple.

Rabbi Meir said that the Tree of Knowledge was a grapevine, "for nothing causes more heartbreak than wine . . ."

Rabbi Nehemiah said the Tree of Knowledge was a fig tree because after the sin, Adam and Eve "knew that they were naked, and they sewed fig leaves and made themselves loincloths." Rabbi Nehemiah posited, "That which caused their downfall, was then used to rectify them."

Rabbi Judah said that the Tree of Knowledge was wheat stalks because "a child knows not how to call out to his father and mother until he has tasted grain."

According to a Midrash, "Rabbi Azariah and Rabbi Yehuda Bar Simon said in the name of Rabbi Yehoshua ben Levi, 'Heaven forbid! The Holy One, blessed be He, never revealed [the identity of] that tree to any person, and He never will.'" Thus, the honor of the tree that would otherwise be tarnished, through no fault of its own, is protected. No one should look at an apple tree, or any other species of tree, and attribute to it the downfall of humanity.

On the contrary, we should celebrate and enjoy the apple for the miracle that it is, in all its varieties and tastes: tart, tender, juicy, sweet, and crisp. Hallelujah, King Apple!

- Interested in the health benefits of apples? Type in the word apples to these links:

    healthline.com

    webmd.com

    eatingwell.com

- Want to try a new apple recipe?

    The pioneerwoman.com

    Delish.com

    Tasteofhome.com

THE BLESSINGS
OF A FRUIT TREE

(Luxury and Pleasure)

And you shall eat and be satisfied and you shall bless Hashem, your God,

for the good land which He has given you.

– DEUTERONOMY 8:10

Flowering plants, known to botanists as angiosperms, consist of more than 250,000 species, the largest group in the plant kingdom. These plants grow seeds inside containers that we call fruits (Greek: angeion, "vessel"; sperma, "seed").

A visit to the countryside in the northern hemisphere in April or May, depending upon where you live, brings you face to face with flowering fruit trees. Anyone who is lucky enough to live among or visit orchard lands knows how special it feels when the trees are in bloom. A manifestation of abundance and blessing is present on every flowering tree. Our love of beauty is triggered when we admire the mosaic of color, bark, earth, and sky.

In the Jewish tradition, flowering fruit trees provide more than an opportunity to enjoy the attractiveness of the trees in bloom, but to praise God with a traditional prayer:

> *Baruch Ata Adonoy Eloheinu Melech ha'olam*
> *shelo chisar ba'olamo davar*
> *u'vara vo b'riyot tovot vi'ilanot tovim*
> *li'hanot bahem b'nei adam*

> *Blessed are you, Lord our God, King of the Universe*
> *for there is nothing lacking in the world at all,*
> *and He created good creatures and good trees,*
> *through which pleasure is brought to the children of Adam*

This springtime prayer encapsulates so much in such few words. Fruit trees, through their beauty, heavenly scents, and produce, bring enormous pleasure to human beings. Although God is obscured in our human experience, even in nature, the fruit tree is one of the wonders of nature that helps us appreciate and stand in awe of God and the Universe.

Wonderful fruits that we can harvest and eat create a feeling of abundance, a sense of gratitude for living in a world where nothing is lacking, and where we can not only meet our needs, but do so with great enjoyment.

The gift of fruit trees also embodies the principle of sharing, a model of how God interacts with human beings. We can emulate God's generosity to us with our fellow human beings. The abundance of fruit produced by trees is easily shared. Not even the most gluttonous person can consume all the fruit of even just one mature healthy tree.

If you have a fruit tree in your own yard, you can watch the tree's flower buds turn into fruit. The buds of each flower are layered with intricate structures that swell and plump, full of energy, infused with the divine, until each unfurls and bursts into blooms. The flowers, delicate patterns of colors with dainty elegance, don't last long. The petals fall off when the flower is fertilized and its ovary starts to grow, turning into the fruit. When fruits ripen, their colors change, with increases in yellow, orange, and red pigments. The initial astringent, bitter composition of the fruit, which protects immature fruits from predators, is replaced by sugars, cell walls swell, and suddenly we can pick and consume what is soft or crisp and as perfectly delicious as any food that we will ever experience. If

The buds of each flower are layered with intricate structures that swell and plump, full of energy, infused with the divine, until each unfurls and bursts into blooms.

unconsumed, the fruit rapidly deteriorates and decomposes so that it can release its seeds. In the case of fruit trees, their seeds are often very hard and range from singular large pits to numerous small seeds of various shapes and sizes.

Witnessing this reproductive cycle of fruits every year provides insight and inspiration for our own lives. We too can produce our own fruits consisting of bountiful good deeds, with positivity towards our environment and fellow human beings. As stated in Deuteronomy (20:19), "A person is like the tree of a field." With strong roots in knowing who we are and what nurtures us best, we can become just as productive as a mature fruit tree year after year. Just as the tree completes its purpose of growing fruit each year, we can grow in our work, relationships, and deeds to fulfill our destiny.

In the Talmud (Taanit 5b), Rabbi Yitzhak, told a parable as follows:

A man was walking through the desert who was hungry, tired, and thirsty. And he found a tree whose fruits were sweet and whose shade was pleasant, and a stream of water flowed beneath it. He ate from the fruits of the tree, drank from the water in the stream, and sat in the shade of the tree. And when he wished to leave, he said: Tree, tree, with what shall I bless you? If I say to you that your fruits should be sweet, your fruits are already sweet; if I say that your shade should be pleasant, your shade is already pleasant; if I say that a stream of water should flow beneath you, a stream of water

already flows beneath you. Rather, I will bless you as follows: May it be God's
will that all saplings which they plant from you be like you.

It feels natural and fulfilling to bless those closest to us. The "fruit" we produce as humans is best shared with our family, friends, co-workers, and neighbors. Fruit spoils quickly. Share what you can as soon as you can to avoid rot and decay. We can give others sustenance through our own healthy and positive good deeds, providing a healthy environment for future generations. When that happens, we feel gratitude throughout our being, throughout our roots, trunk, branches, and leaves. We give thanks for the opportunity for fulfillment, and luxuriate in the preciousness of life.

- Have you ever sent a box of fruit to a friend far away?
- Small yard? Check out dwarf fruit trees
- Do you know about multi-grafted fruit trees? Different varieties on the same tree!

ORLAH

(Discipline and Boundaries)

A child, discipline him with the left hand and draw him closer with the right hand.

– TALMUD, SOTAH, 47A

The Old Testament illuminates the spiritual dimensions of the human being's relationship to fruit trees.

In Leviticus, we are commanded as follows:

> *When you enter the land and plant any tree for food, you shall regard its fruit as forbidden. Three years it shall be forbidden for you, not be eaten. In the fourth year all its fruit shall be set aside for jubilation before the Lord; and only in the fifth year may you use its fruit – that its yield to you may be increased (Lev. 19:23-25).*

This commandment (*mitzvah*), called *orlah*, prohibits eating the fruit of a new tree for three years after it's planted. At first glance, the three-year prohibition might be viewed as a good gardening tip. Three years allows the tree to develop and grow in its natural state untouched and un-weakened by human beings. As stated by the commandment, this may even increase its yield. However, immature fruit is usually not even edible; and in fact, most fruit trees do not even produce fruit during this initial three-year time period. Why then is there a rule that prohibits something that is highly unlikely to occur in the proscribed time period? Does the *mitzvah* of *orlah* have a deeper meaning? It doesn't really make sense as a gardening tip.

The placement of the prohibition of *orlah* in Leviticus is followed by a prohibition of other practices, including soothsaying, witchcraft, tattooing, and other kinds of disfigurement that were common among the Canaanites. A common thread runs through each prohibition. A person's ownership, dominion, and control of their physical body, or that of his or her offspring, is not exclusive, but is rather a joint ownership and enterprise with God. Further, a person's future is not entirely within his or her control, contrary to what the soothsayer or witch might have you believe. Similarly, a grower's selection of where to plant, how much to irrigate and fertilize, and how and when to prune does not fully determine the harvest of the fruit tree. A greater power, clearly beyond the control of the human being, is at work. Thus, *orlah* serves as an acknowledgment and reminder that human beings are not in charge of the myriad forces and interactions of nature.

The rabbinical sages and commentators further explain the meaning of *orlah*. They interpret the root of the term *orlah* to mean "blocked" or "shut off" from our use. Saliently, they note the term *orlah* also appears in Genesis (17:11), referring to the foreskin removed by ritual circumcision. The commentators describe man, in the case of circumcision, an emblem of the Jew's covenant with God, as proactively cut off from a wicked path and bound to the ways of Torah and spirituality, a life in partnership with God by observing God's commandments. Once bound by the covenant with God through ritual circumcision, man possesses the capacity to cling to what is holy and to block himself from evil inclinations.

This concept of spiritual blockage relates back to Adam and Eve's sin of eating fruit from the Tree of Knowledge. The commentators explain that the forbidden fruit was not intended to be eternally prohibited, but that Adam and Eve had to wait until the holy Shabbos to enjoy the fruit. Temptation got the better of them. When they failed to delay their pleasure, the revelation of the complete spirituality present in *Gan Eden* was compromised by their overindulgence. The time we are commanded to wait before eating new fruits stands as a reminder of the time Adam and Eve failed to wait to eat the fruit of the Tree of Knowledge.

Our natural inclination as human beings towards instant gratification undermines and often destroys the spirituality that we might otherwise obtain, creating a wall that separates us from realizing our full potential. All of the earthly blessings, pleasures, and satisfactions known to humankind are ours to enjoy. Yet, sometimes we will buy too much, eat too much, or watch too much television. We might overconsume processed foods, sugar, or alcohol, despite knowing the risks. Yes, we're human. We are going to overdo it some of the time, but do we need to overdo it quite so much? The lesson of Adam and Eve in the Garden teaches that we must exercise discipline and boundaries when it comes to hedonistic impulses.

Consuming what nature and the fruit trees have to offer without thought, without patience, and without self-control is greedy, destructive, and ultimately blocks our spirituality. Life's blessings are not measured by the speediest and most opportunistic consumption. What we consume is best elevated and most enjoyed with self-control, limiting ourselves to what is important.

We are gifted with the luxury of enjoying the pleasures of the physical world and the gift of living with a higher purpose if we also exercise the gifts of discipline and self-control. The fruit tastes better when we wait for it and marvel at its spiritual dimensions. "Its yield to you may be increased" through a pervasive conservation and respect for nature, and by employing an environmental ethic in our everyday lives. As the Lubavitcher Rebbe, Rabbi Menachem Mendel Schneerson, taught in his *Likutei Sichos* (Collected Talks and Letters), "The greatest holiness is that which penetrates the mundane fabric of everyday life, so that even the lowest parts of this physical world are devoted to the 'praise of God.'" Rabbi Abraham Joshua Heschel, the distinguished Jewish philosopher, taught, "Self-respect is the root of discipline. The sense of dignity grows with the ability to say no to oneself."

These wise rabbis knew that living hedonistically, in pursuit of instant gratification, cheapens pleasure and meaning. If we disrespect our physical world by exploiting its natural resources, without discipline, without thought and care, will its yield increase or decrease? The answer is not hidden. The human being's capacity to destroy what grows naturally has run amok; now, can we reverse the trend with discipline and boundaries? If humanity succumbed to its current predicament, after being born into a perfect world, what's to stop us from traveling in the opposite direction, heavenward, while here on earth?

> *If humanity succumbed to its current predicament, after being born into a perfect world, what's to stop us from traveling in the opposite direction, heavenward, while here on earth?*

- Right before you eat your next bite of fruit, try saying this prayer:

Ba-ruch A-tah A-do-noi	*Blessed are You, Lord our God,*
Elo-Hai-Nu Me-lech Ha-o-lam	*King of the Universe*
Bo-Rai Pri Ha Aitz	*Who Creates the fruit of the tree.*

- Interested in planting a backyard fruit tree? See, treefruit.wsu.edu.

TREE OF LIFE

(*Etz Chaim* – Divine Emanations)

The reward for a mitzvah is a mitzvah.

– PIRKEI AVOT, ETHICS OF THE FATHERS, 4:2

L'Chaim, a toast meaning "to life," is part of our religious and secular culture, especially when we propose a toast in celebration of life events. In Jewish circles, the term *Etz Chaim* is also widely known. It means "Tree of Life," and you will see synagogues and Jewish schools so named, not to mention major works of Jewish mysticism. Jewish jewelry often depicts the tree of life on many necklaces. In many synagogues, there is often a wall where an artful tree adorned with leaves is displayed. The names of the founders and contributors to the synagogue are usually engraved on the individual leaves. But what is the origin of these representations of the Tree of Life?

Genesis 2:9 describes God's creation of *Gan Eden*, the Garden of Eden. There are resplendent and fruity trees there, but two trees in particular garner special mention. In the middle of the Garden, Adam encounters the Tree of Life and the Tree of Knowledge of Good and Evil. We have all heard the story of the Tree of Knowledge, where Adam and Eve are forbidden to eat its fruit, but what do we commonly understand about its neighbor, the Tree of Life?

Here is the relevant passage in Genesis concerning these famous trees:

> *Almighty God made every tree that is pleasant to look at and good to eat grow out from the ground. The Tree of Life (grew) in the middle of the garden, and the Tree of Knowledge of good and evil (also grew in the garden).*

Jewish mystics view the Tree of Life as the connection between heaven and earth. According to the Kabbalists, the Tree of Life is represented by an interconnected diagram that joins heaven and earth and God and man. God is both above the ground, permeating the celestial heavens, and below, here on earth, obscured in our physical and material world. The Tree of Life unites the heavenly and the earthly, the spiritual and the material.

Jewish mystics view the Tree of Life as the connection between heaven and earth.

Perhaps more widely invoked, the Tree of Life is often used as a metaphor for the Torah. When the Torah is returned to the ark after it's read on the Holy Shabbos, many congregations chant, *Etz chaim hee l'machazikin bah*, "She is a Tree of Life to those who grasp it, and those who support it." This metaphor derives from Proverbs 3:18. The sages relate that those who "grasp" are the students of Torah who study daily to mine and internalize its Divine wisdom. Those who "support" it are the lay people who donate the money to the rabbis and scholars to ensure Torah study endures. The metaphor is repeated in Proverbs where the "fruit of the righteous" (Proverbs 11:30) and a "healing tongue" (15:4) is also linked to the biblical Tree of Life.

To say "*L'Chaim*" in a meaningful way surely incorporates *Etz Chaim*, and all the difficult to articulate spiritual components of our lives. This may be why doing a good deed is compared to planting a seedling or even planting just a single seed. Every seed, in order to grow, must disintegrate, thus nullifying its own identity, and join with the microbes and nutrients in the soil, to tap into the essence of creation, mother earth herself. The seed or seedling will one day mature into a glorious tree that in turn will produce seeds. Those seeds will become a strand of trees and ultimately, if simply allowed to grow, a magnificent, life-sustaining forest.

For us to perform good deeds, sometimes we must nullify ourselves, putting aside our self-centeredness and greed. We may need to forget ourselves, and our own self-interest, to plant that seed. But when we do, we tap into the Tree of Life for generations to come.

One good deed begets another. Likewise, our positive actions nourish our values. Don't we want to give life to ourselves, our children, and our grandchildren? And thus when we say "*L'Chaim!*" we really mean it. We form part of the *Etz Chaim*, The Tree of Life.

- Think of three good deeds to incorporate into your daily life that may lessen your environmental footprint.
- Call someone up with good cheer that you haven't spoken to in a while.
- Do something nice for your parents, spouse, or children.

THE FOREST OF MOUNT SINAI

(Praying for One's Mission)

It [noble or awakened heart] is said to be present in all beings.
Just as butter is inherent in milk and oil is inherent in a sesame seed,
this soft spot is inherent in you and me.

– PEMA CHODRON, TEACHER, AUTHOR, AND BUDDHIST NUN

———————————

Prayer is salutary. Jews worldwide fast and pray on Yom Kippur each year, also known as the Day of Atonement, invoking the memory of the Ten Martyrs and Rabbi Akiva. Below is a prayer I wrote about praying for one's mission, inspired by Yom Kippur. This prayer also incorporates a famous Midrash about the fox and the fish in the forest. (If inclined, pray in your own way for your and your family's health and for all living things on earth.)

———————————

My Father My King, Master of the Universe, Blessed Creator:

My feet are soiled and tired. I walked 'round and 'round, without purpose, fallen, and sick. I was unforgiving, and bitterness grew, unknowingly, year in, year out.

I forgot those who perished, blown to the four corners of the world, decaying in graves.

While the sword fought with the pen, I lost myself in gluttony, earning wages, polluting the garden, and making little noises.

We blew this way and that in the wind, grasping at the latest fashionable conceit, and tried to distinguish ourselves.

Years later, my bones ache while the womb of the earth seems ever near. Did we leave a warren of prisons and lowly states while shaded by a canopy of loss?

My Father My King, Master of the Universe, Blessed Creator:

On the day we remember the Ten Martyrs, we see Rabbi Akiva walking through the forest. He saw the fox ask the nervous fish, "From what are you fleeing?" They replied, "We are fleeing from the nets that people cast upon us." The fox entreated, "Do you wish to come up onto dry land, and we will live together, just as my ancestors resided with yours?" The fish replied, "You are the one of whom they say, he is the cleverest of animals? You are not clever; you are a fool. If we are afraid in the water, our natural habitat, which gives us life, then how shall we feel in a habitat that causes our death?"

On the day we remember the Ten Martyrs, we shudder, notwithstanding our familiarity with the story, as we see Rabbi Akiva shackled before Roman idolaters, tortured, and death imminent. As the assassins heated their iron combs to flay the great Talmudic sage's flesh, he recited the Shema with a humble, beneficent smile. Asked why, Rabbi Akiva explained to his tormentors that all his life he had read the prayer, "And you shall love your God with all your heart, all your soul, and all your possessions," but was never able to fulfill the obligation to love God with all his soul, until now, as the Roman combs glowed red hot.

The sages teach that when Moses ascended Mount Sinai, summoned to receive the Torah, he saw The Holy One, blessed be He, attaching little crowns to the letters. Moses asked, "Master of the Universe, what remains from giving of the Torah?"

God answered, "There will be a man in the future, at the end of a number of generations, and Akiva ben Joseph is his name. He will interpret heaps and heaps of laws from just the tips of these crowns."

Moses beseeched, "Master, please show him to me!"

God replied, "Turn around!"

Moses sat down behind eight rows of students, not understanding what they were saying, and feeling distressed, until the students asked Rabbi Akiva, "Master, from where do you know this?" and he said to them, "It is a law given to Moses at Sinai," and Moses was comforted.

Holy sages, descendants of the Patriarchs, happy in their wisdom, who gained understanding, worth more than all gold and all treasures, you were each alone when you climbed Mount Sinai. With each step through the forest, you sought pardon, forgiveness, and atonement. You did not run away from your mission. You felt the knife blade of injustice, the terror of exile and inquisition, the depths of cold, fear, rage, and chaos. Yet you climbed toward the light, toward mercy, love, and compassion, and toward a vision of redemption.

My Father My King, Master of the Universe, Blessed Creator:

I pray for my mission; may I walk in the forest of my Mount Sinai. I need to take a simple step, then another, and another. The trees will guide my way. My wounds will heal. I will breathe the air, thanks to the trees. The air will penetrate my heart with wonder and joy. Let me start at the beginning. Let me discover, understand, and heed the mandate to Adam to be careful not to destroy the trees that the Holy Master of the Universe created, to understand balance, oneness, the preciousness of

I pray for my mission

each forest, and the majesty of each tree. Can I keep growing like the trees, full of sap in the spring, stretching heavenward, while only limited by the gravity, time, and space found in nature?

- Plan a hike in an old-growth forest. While there, pray in your own way.

THE NEW YEAR
FOR TREES

(*Tu B'Shvat* – Rebirth)

For in the tree is hope. If it is felled, it will sprout again,

and that the tender branch thereof will not cease.

– JOB 14:7

On the Jewish calendar, the fifteenth day of the month of Shevat is the holiday of *Tu B'Shvat*, the New Year for Trees. The holiday, as currently celebrated, has elements of the secular Earth Day and Arbor Day, as Jews in the Land of Israel and throughout the world plant trees and promote environmental awareness on this holiday. However, the origin of *Tu B'Shvat* is as ancient as the oral Torah given to Moses on Mount Sinai. *Tu B'Shvat* marks the date for calculating the agricultural cycle for the purpose of tithing. Trees in Israel are awakening on *Tu B'Shvat* from their winter slumber as the moisture and nutrients accumulated in the soil during the winter months begin to flow up and outward. The vitality of the trees is plainly visible to everyone as the trees begin their new growth for the year. The holiday thus symbolizes the never-ending cycle of nature. The rebirth and revitalization of the trees in Israel is an annual cause for joyous celebration and for blessing God, the Creator of the Universe.

Observant Jews celebrate the New Year for Trees by reciting a blessing and eating ripe fruits, especially, when available, ones that were traditionally grown in biblical times in Israel: olives, dates, grapes, figs, and pomegranates. Yet, *Tu B'Shvat* is the day when the trees in Israel begin their growth cycle for another year, so the fruit of these trees isn't even yet ready. The fruit hasn't fully formed, let alone ripened sufficiently to pick and consume. As the learned sages point out, within this seeming contradiction is an important lesson. The reason Jews commemorate the day the sap begins to flow by eating ripe fruit is because the beauty of the fruit's appearance, smell, and taste demonstrates unequivocally the greatness and importance of the potential of each tree. As a person is compared to "a tree of the field," the New Year for Trees is also a day for us to recognize the greatness and potential in each of us. With this mindset, can we avoid recognizing our own potential when we see and smell beautifully ripe and luxurious fruit right in front of our eyes and noses?

However, the question arises—how do we reach our full potential? The great Jewish sages tell us the answer is through labor and toil. If we plant a seed or a seedling, it takes many years to grow to produce fruit. Throughout that time period, especially during the young fruit tree's most formative years, the seedling will need proper conditions to grow and also need protection from weeds, birds, and other animals. As the sages have stated, "Even the king is subservient to the soil." Thus, to reach our full potential, the learned sages tell us that we must begin to work even when we can only see potential; even though the time for harvesting is far, far away. To enjoy the fruits of our labors takes dedication, effort, and vigilance, sometimes over a lengthy passage of time.

In Psalms, specific mention is made of a palm tree that does not produce its fruits for seventy years after planting. This emphasizes the point that growing trees is not like growing grain. Wheat and barley are planted and harvested within months. Trees take much greater patience and effort, but once well established, trees can produce their fruits for years. Perhaps this is why the refrain, "The tzaddik [righteous person] who blossoms like a palm tree" refers to someone who has reached the age of seventy.

Given that it may take many years to enjoy the fruit of our labors, the holy rabbis say that there is no time to waste. Every day that we procrastinate is a day that has lost its purpose and lessened our potential. No one is going to do your work for you. And no one can say how long you will have to accomplish your tasks. Only you can complete your mission. It takes effort to make your potential a reality. Every moment contains wonderful potential.

Another distinction between fruits and grains is that wheat and barley represent the necessities of life while fruit represents luxury. Fruit refreshes the soul. God has given us more than what we need to merely survive. Fruit provides inspiration for our mission. What's better than a freshly picked, perfectly ripe strawberry, peach, or apricot? Bite in and enjoy life. Let's delight in the fruits of our labors, especially its sweetness. Anticipating the fruits of our labors, let's go about our workday with joy.

What's better than a freshly picked, perfectly ripe strawberry, peach, or apricot?

Although we celebrate the New Year for Trees only once a year, the lessons of the holiday should help us spring out of bed each day, giving thanks for having awoken, and for being given another day to feel inspired, to get to work, and to do good deeds.

- Do you live near a springtime blossom trail? Want to take an inspiring field trip? See:

    Dottedglobe.com/bestspring-flowers-usa/
    visitvisalia.com
    goblossomtrail.com
    visityakima.com
    enjoyillinois.com

- Try a new fruit.

- Organize a school field trip to a local park to collect litter.

- Pot a young tree seedling that is growing too close to its mother tree.

THE CAROB TREE

(Old Age and Retirement)

Think a year ahead, plant rice. Think ten years ahead, plant trees.
Think one hundred years ahead, educate the people.

– CONFUCIUS, PHILOSOPHER, POLITICIAN, AND POET

The sages of the Talmud relate the story of the old man who was planting a seedling. A young man passed by and asked what he was planting. The old man told the young one that he was planting a carob tree. The youth asked critically, "Don't you know that it takes seventy years for a carob tree to bear fruit?" "That's okay," said the old man. "Just as others planted for me, I plant for future generations."

Our penchant for instant gratification seems to suggest that efforts that do not produce immediate results are meaningless. We seek a pay-off right now. The young man questioned the justification for the old man's toil because the old man would not be around to enjoy the fruits of his labor. A carob tree seedling took so long to grow and bear fruit that planting it seemed insignificant, valueless, and irrelevant. Why go to the trouble?

Additionally, sometimes we look at years or even decades of our own hard work and question ourselves. We wonder if we accomplished anything. After years of great effort, zeal and sacrifice, the results seem ambiguous, hard to grasp, like a dream. We tried so hard to do the right thing, but did it matter?

In hindsight, we might see ourselves as a donkey plodding after a carrot dangled on a string. The dangling carrot keeps the donkey moving forward. We never attained what we wanted just like the carrot was always out of the donkey's reach. We always had to clear another hurdle. We needed to finish high school to go to college or get a job. We needed to get a car. We needed to get a boyfriend or girlfriend. We needed to finish college. We needed to get an advanced degree. We needed to get a promotion. We needed to get married, to buy a house, to have children, to go on a vacation, to buy a better house, to save for our children's educations. Even upon accomplishing the goal at hand, fulfillment remained out of reach. If only I had a car, a boyfriend or a girlfriend, a college degree, a good job, a better job, life would be as it should be. But a new obstacle repeatedly emerged and an inner voice told us that contentment lay just around the corner. We didn't realize that when one journey was completed, we needed another one.

The clock keeps ticking, and we finally retire. We think it is time to slow down, to live as comfortably as possible, as long as the money lasts. We look back and we wonder why we flocked to the latest fashion, fad, and novelty. The latest electronic gizmo came out and we all needed to get one. We sought wealth for its own sake, and now we feel surrounded by much more stuff than we can ever need or consume. We feel a nagging dissatisfaction, as we eventually start looking over our shoulder, wondering when the next doctor's appointment will be our last, frustrated at the long line at the pharmacy and all the insurance paperwork.

The fact is that our souls do not care about material success, the accumulation of wealth, and social status. Our real wealth is not measured in stock accounts or rental properties, vacation timeshares, or sleek automobiles. The billionaire is in no way superior to the person of average means who is connected to nature and the environment, to loved ones, and to a healthy community.

Further, our souls do not retire. While our physical bodies weaken, our souls are timeless, never aging, living on, seeking light, and wanting so much to give. The contemporary concept of retirement suggests that we stop living at an arbitrary age and spend years that could otherwise be fruitful and productive, preparing to die.

The billionaire is in no way superior to the person of average means who is connected to nature and the environment, to loved ones, and to a healthy community.

If a person's life is compared to that of a tree, consider that the older the tree, the more human respect it engenders with its aesthetic beauty, and the more bountiful its fruit. Its branches provide a habitat for the birds, shade for our home, and a jungle gym for children to climb. Scientists in the fields of botany, biology, and ecology have concluded that older trees take in more atmospheric carbon and release more oxygen far more prodigiously than younger ones. Just as trees become more powerful and beneficial in these respects as they age, so does the human soul. The spirituality of the aged is at its peak level of creativity. The elderly understand that health is the number one priority because life is precious, and that with age comes wisdom. Old age is not a liability, despite cultural messages to the contrary.

If we are older, we possess a great opportunity to educate the young. If we are older, we enjoy great credibility due to our wisdom and experience. Our voices will be heard and our voices are persuasive. To advocate for nature, to participate in land preservation, reforestation, and the fight for environmental sustainability are all good deeds that affect the entire world. Good deeds last forever.

In our senior years, we can replenish ourselves, just like old trees cycle carbon with their leaves, with good deeds for the earth. The best way for the elderly to expand their spirits is to experience nature, to get outside on the trail, and to speak for the trees. Tzedakah, the word commonly used to denote charity, literally means justice and righteousness. We can realize the utmost importance of our mission to cultivate, preserve, guard, educate, refine, sustain, persuade, and set an example with tzedakah, giving tzedakah for succeeding generations and providing tzedakah for the earth. We are able to care about the future in the present moment. We are able to feel satisfaction in our tasks and our labors, even if the gratification seems delayed or completely out of our reach. We can do the right thing. Our souls know it when we do. It is never too late to do the right thing. We can act with generosity for succeeding generations.

Rest assured, the seeds we plant now will have time enough to grow. Accomplishments are not necessarily valued in the moment, or even realized during our own lifetimes. It may take seventy years, but the carob trees planted today will fulfill their destiny. We may best fulfill our own destiny if we do what we can right now, for the benefit of our souls, and for the collective soul of humanity, to cultivate, preserve, and guard our precious garden.

- Is someone you know retiring soon? Give a gift of a tree.
- Do you know a senior with limited mobility who you can help get outdoors?
- Sit under a shade tree, close your eyes, take a few deep breaths, and imagine your senior years—what do you see?

THE OLD CATALPA

(Loving a Favorite Tree)

Trees and plants have a language of their own.

– BAAL SHEM TOV

I thank that I shall never see a poem lovely as a tree.

– JOYCE KILMER, TREES AND OTHER POEMS, 1914

My favorite chapter in the first book of this series, *The Spiritual Gardener*, wasn't about gardening, but rather about my favorite tree, a catalpa. This tree was beloved by me, my family, and enjoyed by many a summer's guest who luxuriated in its shade. I couldn't write a book about trees without including this chapter, *The Old Catalpa*. I hope you enjoy reading it as much as I enjoyed writing it.

The old catalpa tree was a haven for the birds each spring. As the catalpa's leaves grew again, songbirds established their nests which were soon hidden by the catalpa's floppy green leaves. The nestlings became all but invisible, although their chirping and their parents' frequent excursions to bring food to the nests confirmed their presence. April often brought a couple of teaser days when the clouds parted and the temperature warmed enough to sit outside and soak in the sun's warmth while listening to the constant cries for food from the baby birds hidden inside the catalpa's canopy.

The old catalpa was also a jungle gym for children, mostly boys around age nine or ten, who could not resist climbing the trunk starting where it had a big bump to ascend to its platform where the main branches began. Eventually, the tree started growing some weeds up there where the leaves pooled up and a neighborhood raccoon left some scat. The catalpa also had lots of holes higher up where the woodpeckers hollowed out its branches, but the old tree continued to grow majestically year after year. The tree's jasmine-scented flowers always bloomed late, and when a late July windstorm timed it just right, the white flowers fell in mass and covered the grass below like a summer's snow. Sitting between the house and the afternoon sun, the catalpa was the home's air conditioner, providing needed shade during the hottest afternoons of August and September. In November and December, the catalpa made a huge

the white flowers fell in mass and covered the grass below like a summer's snow.

mess when all the leaves came down, and it was a hassle to rake up all the leaves, but it forced us outside to get some exercise when we would otherwise be homebound on cold and wet winter days.

When a big catalpa branch came down with a loud, earth-shaking boom, I was on the other side of the house mowing the lawn with the John Deere. I had just mowed the catalpa side of the yard minutes before. I heard a very loud crash. I had no idea what it was. Coming around the house, the catalpa's largest branch sheared off the main part of the tree, bringing down other branches with it. Curiously, the most vulnerable-looking spots where the woodpeckers had carved out holes were still intact, but it was clear that the tree was a hazard and that we were lucky it had not fallen on anyone. We had not realized how dangerous it was, but we loved that tree so we had turned a blind eye to how it had rotted as it continued to grow. It was a hazard and we needed to take it out. We were so sorry to see it go that we paid a pretty penny to the local nursery to order us another one and we planted the new little tree as close as we could to where the old catalpa had stood.

The old catalpa had transformed that part of the yard from something barren into a friendly and beautiful environment that had something for everyone, a home for the birds, a playground for the children, and a cooling shade for the house. The yard looked empty without it, even when we planted the new little catalpa. We knew that it would take years and years for the new catalpa to rival the old one.

A culture that celebrates youthful vitality, viewing old age as a liability, is making a big mistake. It is true that physically we will weaken, decay, and break, just like an old tree. But our old catalpa was at its most majestic and beneficent in its old age. The strength of its branches had weakened and its days were numbered, but the soul of that tree, and what it provided in its environment, grew richer and more valuable each year, until it finally crashed.

No matter how diseased and hollow the old catalpa became, its leaves yearned for nourishment every spring and it grew again and again, dignified and beautiful. As we age, we need not retire from any meaningful pursuit. It may hurt our arthritic necks a little more each year to fulfill our mission, but we know what we are doing and how to do it, and we finally have more time to engage in activities that are priceless. Just as the catalpa's leaves sought the sun, we seek relevance.

We may find seedlings from our trees scattered about in our gardens. Rather than pulling them like weeds, let's give them their own pot. When they are ready, after a year or two of care, let's remove them from their container and plant them in the yard in a good spot or gift them to someone who thinks he or she knows where they should go. Additionally, we can take cuttings from our catalpas and rhododendrons, or any deciduous tree or perennial shrub of our choice, dip them in a little root hormone, pot them gently, make sure they are watered in summer, and keep the pots sheltered and away from the harshest winter storms. By spring we will have new trees and shrubs that sport new growth;

that are readily available to beautify a yard, please the eye, create a playground, provide an environment for living creatures, and turn the barren into the cultivated.

- Do you have a favorite tree?
- How do you care for mature trees? See:

  Canopy.org

  Wikihow.com

ACKNOWLEDGEMENTS

It was wonderfully valuable to see the comments and reactions of a handful of readers who volunteered to read this manuscript before it was edited. I sincerely thank each of you for your time and suggestions, with special thanks to Marian Schwartz who also kindly shared her wonderful photography.

This book is my second collaboration with Howard VanEs from Let's Write Books, Inc. I am truly grateful for his vision, enthusiasm, humor, and guidance. And a grateful thank you to his publishing team as well!

Lastly, a huge thank you to Steve and Giovanna Franklin, for their kind generosity in sponsoring this book and for their commitment to encouraging a healthy and sustainable environment.

"Mountains are not esteemed because they are high,

but because they have trees."

JAPANESE PROVERB

We are proud to support this very beautiful tribute to nature, and
encourage everyone, particularly those like us who are surrounded
by majestic forests in the Pacific Northwest, to read and be inspired by
The Spiritual Forest. Let's all heed Andy's brilliantly written call to action!

STEVE & GIOVANNA FRANKLIN

BECKER | FRANKLIN | ROVANG PLLC
INJURY LAWYERS

ABOUT THE AUTHOR

Andy Becker is a writer, gardener, and lifetime learner, who lives in Western Washington among the cedar trees with his wife Donna and their two dogs, Nova and Splash. Andy was a successful small-town lawyer who found respite from the vicissitudes of fighting for the little guy against insurance companies by gardening, hiking, and camping with his family,  and by expanding his spirituality through Judaism. During his early years of gardening, he was often frustrated, beset by rocky soil, hills, and too many slugs and deer. Despite these challenges, Andy has never failed to grow vegetables every spring and summer. His current garden includes a greenhouse, eight raised beds, a thirty-yard vegetable bed, and a forty-yard stretch of raspberry vines.

His first published book, *The Spiritual Gardener: Insights from the Jewish Tradition to Help Your Garden Grow,* is an illustrated gift book coupling spiritual themes with gardening tasks to inspire gardening and well-being. *The Spiritual Gardener* won the New York City Big Book Award in the Home and Garden category.

Andy's second book, *Cracking an Egg*, is a humorous and heartfelt look at early childhood experiences growing up in the 1960s.

Andy's third book and debut novel, *The Kissing Rabbi: Lust, Betrayal, and a Community Turned Inside Out*, is the first #MeToo novel where the antagonist is a young ultra-orthodox rabbi. After building a vibrant community from scratch, the rabbi botches his misguided attempts at the seduction of several congregants and creates a scandal that rocks the community. *The Kissing Rabbi* won a First Place Chanticleer Mark Twain Award for humor and satire.

If you read and like any of Andy's books, please post a favorable review online. For more information about Andy's books, see **www.andybecker.life**. Write directly to Andy at **andybecker.life@gmail.com**

Made in the USA
Las Vegas, NV
13 November 2022

59347057R00077